THE "BIG BOOK OF BIEBER

TRIUMPH
BOOKS

This book is available in quantity at special discounts for your group or organization. For further information, contact:

Triumph Books LLC
542 South Dearborn Street
Suite 750
Chicago, Illinois 60605
(312) 939-3330
Fax (312) 663-3557
www.triumphbooks.com

Printed in U.S.A.

ISBN: 978-1-60078-713-3

Content developed and packaged by Rockett Media, Inc.
Writer: Katy Sprinkel
Editor: Bob Baker
Design and page production: Andrew Burwell
Cover design: Preston Pisellini
All photos courtesy of Getty Images unless otherwise noted.

THE BIG BOOK OF BIEBER

Chapter 1:

ON TOP OF
THE WORLD

Chapter 1:
ON TOP OF THE WORLD

Justin Bieber is not your typical teenager. In fact, he's not even your typical recording artist. He's never acted on Nickelodeon. He never had a show on the Disney Channel. He doesn't have a blond alter ego—well, at least when he's not pranking his audience. He isn't a boy-bander or a Jonas Brother or even a little bit Raven.

What he is, however, is the first bona fide Internet musical success story. Armed with a video camera and a computer, he leveraged his best asset—his natural talent—all the way to superstardom.

When Justin's mom, Pattie, started posting videos on YouTube of Justin singing in 2007, it was because she wanted to share them with family members. But the world stood up and took notice. Before long, "kidrauhl," his YouTube channel, was getting hits from random strangers—lots of them!

One of those viewers was Scooter Braun, an Atlanta-based party promoter and fledgling music producer. He saw something special in the baby-faced Canadian singer—a kid who could belt an anthem from Aretha Franklin as well as master the neo-soul of contemporary pop artists like Chris Brown and Lil Bow Wow.

Braun was sure he had found lightning in a bottle. He just had to be Justin's manager. But actually signing him was another story. It took a lot to convince Pattie. She was concerned about thrusting her young son into the cutthroat recording industry, but after a long talk about family and morals Braun finally persuaded her that he had Justin's best interests at heart. They got straight to work boosting his Internet numbers even further and getting his name out to radio stations and music executives. A recording contract soon followed.

Flash forward to 2011. Justin has conquered the Internet, the music world, and Hollywood. His concert ticket sales have exceeded even generous expectations. His record sales are sky-high. His branding empire is big business. He even published his own memoir, which quickly became a best-seller.

He's won every award from the AMA to the VMA. In 2010 he was one of Barbara Walters' Most Fascinating People; in 2011,

$53 MILLION

Justin's reported earnings in 2010, making him the second-highest earner on Forbes' list of best-paid celebrities. He trails only fashion rebel and fellow recording artist Lady Gaga.

THIS DAY IN JB-ISTORY

Pattie Mallette posts the first video of Justin on YouTube: his cover of "So Sick" by Ne-Yo.

JANUARY 19, 2007

Justin Bieber backstage at the 2010 American Music Awards held at Nokia Theatre L.A. Live on November 21, 2010 in Los Angeles, California.

Musician Justin Bieber (L) and actor
Paul Rudd at the 2011 MTV Video Music

WHO AM I?

Think you know everything about Justin Bieber? Our mystery person is one of the true Beliebers. See if you can guess who it is by using the hints below.

- I was born on April 3, 1976.
- I am French-Canadian.
- My middle name is Lynn.
- I have one child.
- Justin has described me as "the person most responsible for [his] success."

one of Forbes' Highest Paid Celebrities. He's been honored as a humanitarian. Heck, he's even sung at the White House—three times!

He's broken iTunes download records, YouTube records, and has generated never-before-seen Twitter numbers. One employee of the social-networking site remarked that the company uses three percent of its servers just for Justin and his Twitter followers.

His branding empire is big business, too. He's got his face on everything from fragrances to cosmetics to book covers and Silly Bandz. And much of the profits from his merchandise go straight to his favorite charities.

His personal charitable contributions have been massive, and he has sparked a legion of fans to make change within their own communities. His philanthropic efforts earned him an award from Do Something, the nation's largest organization promoting volunteerism among younger generations.

TWITTER-PATED:

4 years ago I started this account www.youtube.com/kidrauhl - thanks for taking this ride with me. #wearejustgettingstarted #neversaynever

JANUARY 16, 2010

Chapter 1:
ON TOP OF THE WORLD

Add role model to his list of accomplishments. He acknowledges the power of music to be persuasive, and he takes the platform he has with his fans seriously. "I'm looking forward to influencing others in a positive way. My message is you can do anything if you just put your mind to it," he says on his official Web site.

With a philosophy like that, it's easy to see that he's just getting started. He has many other goals yet to conquer. He wants to graduate from college. "I grew up below the poverty line; I didn't have as much as other people did. I think it made me stronger as a person [and] it built my character. Now I have a 4.0 grade point average and I want to go to college and just become a better person," he said on his Web site.

> ### SAY WHAT?
>
> *"[This is] just the beginning. There's so much more in store for the future."*
>
> —*Usher, describing Justin's potential to MTV News*

• Justin Bieber performs on stage at the Koenig-Pilsener-Arena on March 26, 2011, in Oberhausen, Germany.

ANSWER: *PATTIE MALLETTE*

Chapter 1:
ON TOP OF THE WORLD

He wants to act in a movie. (No, his concert documentary *Justin Bieber: Never Say Never* doesn't count.) He also wants to win a Grammy. He wants to make an impact on the world.

So many amazing things have come to Justin already but he constantly strives to achieve more. And above all, he keeps in mind that it is all about the fans. "I'll never forget that none of this would have happened without you," he wrote in the introduction to his book, *First Step 2 Forever*. And that's no lip service. Justin stays in constant contact with his fans via Twitter and other social media. He also puts the fans front and center in all of his performances.

"This is just the beginning," he wrote in his book. With the incredible talent, drive, and strength of character that Justin has shown in his career thus far, there's no doubt: the sky's the limit.

> **QUOTABLE** *JUSTIN*
>
> *"It's been pretty amazing. I'm really glad that I've just been able to do what I love."*
>
> **—Justin describing his career to CNN**

MATCH-MAKING

Sometimes it's a numbers game. Can you match Justin's accomplishments with their numbers?

A: The highest Justin has charted on the Billboard Hot 100	2
B: The number of full-length albums Justin has released	3
C: The number of American Music Awards Justin won in 2010	4
D: Box-office ranking for *Justin Bieber: Never Say Never* in its opening weekend	5

Answers: A-5, B-3, C-4, D-2

Chapter 2:
O CANADA!

Chapter 2:
O CANADA!

Stratford, Ontario, Canada, is, by all counts, a beautiful place to grow up. A small community located in southwest Ontario, it is a quiet little burg situated smack dab in the middle of three major cities: Toronto, Ontario; Detroit, Michigan; and Buffalo, New York.

But don't let all that urban influence fool you. Stratford has a charm all its own. Billed as "Canada's Premier Arts Town," Stratford is home to Canada's largest Shakespeare festival. By rights, it's how the town got its name to begin with. It was named after William Shakespeare's birthplace in England: Stratford-Upon-Avon.

Stratford's reputation as an artistic outpost is inarguable, and it is also known for its vast array of galleries, music venues, and theatres. A town of about 30,000 residents, it has produced many impressive talents over the years, but perhaps none bigger than its most recent export: Justin Bieber.

"Canada is an awesome country in general, and Stratford is an excellent place to call home," writes Bieber in *First Step 2 Forever*. "The people are nice, but not easily impressed."

Born March 1, 1994, in Stratford, Justin Drew Bieber was born to parents Pattie Mallette and Jeremy Bieber. Though his parents split when he was only 10 months old, his home life was a happy one. (And he still has a good relationship with his dad, by the way.)

To hear him tell it, he was just a regular Canadian kid. "I love hockey, maple syrup, and Caramilk bars," he writes in *First Step 2 Forever*. He hung out with his friends, skateboarding, telling jokes, playing soccer

> ### DID YOU KNOW?
> *"O Canada" is not just the name of this chapter—it's the name of Canada's national anthem!*

JUSTIN'S FAVORITE THINGS!

CARAMILK BARS. THIS BELOVED CANADIAN CANDY IS ONE OF JUSTIN'S FAVORITES. COMPARABLE TO ITS AMERICAN COUNTERPART, CARAMELLO, IT'S A CHOCOLATE BAR FILLED WITH CARAMEL. YUM!

Justin performs for band camp students at Seminole High School in Sanford, Florida, in August 2010.

Usher and Justin Bieber arrive at Nickelodeon's 2009 Kids' Choice Awards at UCLA's Pauley Pavilion on March 28, 2009, in Westwood, California.

HIT THE ROAD

There are plenty of reasons to visit Stratford in its own right, but for the die-hard Bieber fan, visiting the city is a must. Luckily, the city of Stratford has produced a "Bieber-iffic! Map to Stratford" that serves as a guidebook to some of Justin's favorite haunts in his hometown. (You can download it at www.visitstratford.ca/justin.) Some highlights from Justin's hometown include:

City Hall. This is the spot where Justin performed his first-ever recorded song. It was featured on a CD called *Set a Place at Your Table III*, a charity album benefitting a local food bank.

King's Buffet. The site of Justin's first date! Lucky for us it didn't go so well.

Kiwanis Community Centre. Site of Stratford Star, the singing competition that put Justin's ambition into overdrive.

Swiss Chalet. During Justin's *Rolling Stone* cover shoot, he told the magazine that if he could eat any meal anywhere in the world, he wanted the quarter chicken at this local restaurant. Why? Because "it's so good," he replied.

and basketball, and—like most every Canadian boy—hockey was king. Justin played center forward on his local team, the Stratford Warriors. Whether it was a stick and a puck, a skateboard, a basketball, or a soccer ball, he just loved being active.

Sports were far from his only love, however. From an early age, he showed a keen interest in something that would take him much further: music. In a revealing scene in *Justin Bieber: Never Say Never*, family videos capture a very auspicious moment in his childhood. It depicts a young Justin sitting by the Christmas tree. His eyes light up as he opens the present: a bongo drum. He begins banging on it enthusiastically, putting on a show for the crowd surrounding him. As a fledgling drummer, he's not half bad. As a fledgling entertainer? You can tell he's got it.

"Where does this talent come from? Can he play drums?" asked incredulous friend

QUOTABLE JUSTIN

"Canada's the best country in the world."
—Justin to *Rolling Stone*, when asked if he considers becoming an American citizen

Chapter 2:
O CANADA!

and neighbor, Nathan MacKay. "Man, you gotta get this kid a kit!" he exclaimed.

"I always knew Justin was gifted. Even as a one-year-old who was barely standing, I remember him banging on tables, banging in rhythm," Mallette echoed to *Vanity Fair*.

In the family home, there was always music. If Pattie wasn't playing it on the radio, there were musicians in the house. Many of her friends were musicians and played in the praise band at their local church. In an effort to encourage his apparent musicality, they encouraged Justin to join in with them. Quick to bang on a drum, he played happily along with the music. "Sometimes the percussionist would let me play with the various noisemakers. When he saw that I wanted to play—not just play—he'd let me sit on his knee while he played on the drum kit," Justin writes in his memoir. "After a while, he handed me the sticks and let me have a go at it."

Surrounded by music at home and church, Justin was continually learning. "When I listened to music in church, I could feel the harmonies hanging in the air like humidity. It wasn't an issue of learning it exactly: it was more as if the music soaked in through my skin," he wrote in *First Step 2 Forever*.

It wasn't long before Justin's curiosity led him to new musical instruments. By the time he was able to lift it, he started playing the guitar. He also learned the piano. It turned out Justin had an ear for music, and he would often play songs he had heard on the radio from memory. There wasn't enough money to go around for music lessons, but Justin was thriving on his own as a self-taught musician. He simply had a knack for it.

"Mom couldn't afford lessons for me, but I knew what I wanted the music to sound like. I

JUSTIN'S STOOD HERE!

THIS DAY IN JB-ISTORY
Justin Drew Bieber enters the world!

MARCH 1, 1994

AVON THEATRE. ONE OF THE OLDEST LANDMARKS IN STRATFORD, THIS IS THE SITE WHERE JUSTIN DID HIS MOST FREQUENT PERFORMING. HE ONCE GOT $100 FROM A PASSERBY!

Singer Justin Bieber (R) and mother Pattie Mallette arrives at the 52nd Annual GRAMMY Awards held at Staples Center on January 31, 2010, in Los Angeles, California.

Chapter 2:
O CANADA!

could feel it when the chords and melody fit together, the same way you can feel it when your shoes are on the wrong feet," he wrote in his autobiography.

As much as he loved playing instruments, it was the sounds of singing that most often filled their household. With the radio on, Pattie and Justin would belt out the current hits. Their tastes were eclectic—everything from contemporary R&B acts like Boyz II Men to singer-songwriters like Edwin McCain. Pattie also introduced Justin to some of her old favorites, such as the Beatles and Aretha Franklin. There is no doubt it was Pattie's influence that helped Justin shape his own musical pedigree. Perhaps that's why Justin is so uncategorizable; he just loves music, pure and simple.

All that music was enriching, sure, but it was all for fun—wasn't it? Justin still attended Stratford Northwestern Public School and played after school and did his homework like any other student. (For the record: he liked English. Math? Not so much.) But at age 12, he made a decision to enter a local talent contest—a decision that would change the course of his life forever.

> **TRUE / NOT TRUE?**
>
> *Justin can speak French.*
>
> True: he attended French immersion school in Stratford.

PATTIE MALLETTE:
KEEPING THE FAITH

Pattie Mallette will be the first person to tell you that she hasn't always had it easy. There were times in her life when she felt she had nowhere to turn. There were times when she felt like giving up entirely. But after struggles in her early life, she found faith in herself and in religion. Faith in God is just one of the many things that she's passed on to her son.

In the tumultuous world of entertainment, she believes it's what keeps her—and her son—grounded. "I keep reminding him that he is here for a reason, that as much as it might look like it, it's not all about him, and that God has given him his gifts and talents for a reason, and to seek Him for what that is," she told journalist Adam Holz.

Singer Justin Bieber (R) and mother Pattie Mallette pose for pictures with the Stanley Cup before performing on NBC's *TODAY Show* on June 4, 2010, in New York City.

Justin Bieber performs on the street August 20, 2007, in Stratford, Canada.

TEST YOUR STRATFORD IQ

Sure, you know a lot about Justin, but what about where he comes from? Test your knowledge of Stratford, Ontario, with this brain-busting quiz.

1. What is the name of the annual Shakespeare Festival that takes place in Stratford?

A: The Royal Stratford Shakespeare Festival

B: The Stratford Shakespeare Festival

C: The Stratford Festival of Shakespeare

D: The Royal Theatre Festival

2. What bird, commonly found among the parks and gardens of Stratford, is the town's honorary animal ambassador?

A: Goose

B: Crane

C: Flamingo

D: Swan

3. In what year was Stratford officially established as a city?

A: 1820

B: 1846

C: 1854

D: 1871

4. Stratford is located upon the banks of which river?

A: The Avon River

B: The Little Thames

C: The Huron River

D: The Blue River

5. In what county is Stratford located?

A: Sydney

B: Canberra

C: Melbourne

D: Perth

6. Which famous inventor once worked in Stratford as a telegraph operator for the Grand Trunk Railway?

A: Alexander Graham Bell

B: Thomas Edison

C: Samuel Morse

D: Benjamin Franklin

7. What is the name of the Ontario Hockey Association team based in Stratford?

A: Siskins

B: Sugar Kings

C: Cullitons

D: Winterhawks

Answers: 1-A, 2-D, 3-C, 4-A, 5-D, 6-B, 7-C

Chapter 3:

STRATFORD STAR(T)

Chapter 3:
STRATFORD STAR(T)

The wheels were turning. Singing, which had become an enjoyable leisure-time activity for Justin, was getting increasingly fun. Still, it was something he kept to himself. By all outward appearances, Justin was a fun-loving little boy with a boundless energy that he funneled into any and every sport he could find.

Stratford's emphasis as an arts community no doubt played a role in what came next. The town announced that in January 2007 it would hold a singing

competition in the mold of

American Idol, the popular television program that has launched recording careers for many amateur singers, including Carrie Underwood, Jennifer Hudson, Kelly Clarkson, and Adam Lambert. The reality-show competition has long had a huge audience—perhaps because the audience is so integral to the elimination process. Viewers are asked each week to vote on which contestant they want to keep around, and the singer with the least number of votes is sent home.

The competition was put on by the local YMCA, a spot where Justin frequently played basketball. Perhaps he saw the flyers there and thought, *Why not?* However it went, he decided to enter the competition. Even among the local participants in the Stratford Star contest, he was different. He had no formal training. He had not participated in a choir or other singing group. He was considerably younger—just 12 years old. And perhaps most striking of all, he had never before performed in public.

It was a lot to overcome for young Justin, but as soon as he opened his mouth

---

UNDER THE INFLUENCE

American Idol has no doubt influenced Justin. He posted a cover of Idol alum **Elliot Yamin's** *song "Wait for You" on the kidrauhl YouTube channel.*

VOCABULARY
Busker (ˈbəs·ker)

A person who performs or entertains in public in exchange for audience donations.

Singer Justin Bieber attends the launch party for Vevo, a premium music video and entertainment experience, created by Universal Music Group, Sony Music Entertainment, and YouTube, in New York, on Tuesday, Dec. 8, 2009.

Singer Justin Bieber and musician Taylor Swift attend the 2011 Teen Choice Awards at Gibson Universal Amphitheatre on August 7, 2011, in Universal City, California.

BEHIND THE MUSIC

The Stratford Star contest was a major turning point in Justin's musical life. Everybody knows that Justin, just 12 years old, came in second in the contest. Or do they?

Actually, the contest came down to the final three—Kristen Hawley, Leah Keeley, and Justin. As the drum rolled the winner of the 2007 Stratford Star was...Kristen Hawley. But second and third places were never announced. So Justin could have been second or third.

Perhaps we'll never know for sure which way the votes went. But one thing is certain: Justin is certainly first in our hearts!

and that big voice rang out, people knew he was for real. As the course of the four-week competition went on, Justin was hanging tight. He had sung a wide variety of songs, from Matchbox 20 to Alicia Keys to Sarah McLachlan to Stevie Wonder.

He made it all the way to the finals but ultimately missed out on the grand prize. "We knew there was something special, but we thought 'Give him a couple years with voice training and he would have the whole package.' He was definitely up for the challenge and he had the charisma, he just didn't have the experience," YMCA CEO Mimi Price told the *Toronto Star*. Still, it was a watershed moment for the young musician, whose first performances were enthusiastically received.

By this time an ace on the guitar, he began taking his act to the streets of

QUOTABLE JUSTIN

"Kids had no idea I did music."

—Justin on his "secret" talent, in *First Step 2 Forever*

Chapter 3:
STRATFORD STAR(T)

Stratford. He could often be found busking in front of the Avon Theatre during the town's summer tourist season. Still covering other artists, his list of songs was growing by the day. On any given day, you might hear anything from country groups like Rascal Flatts to Christian artists like Jennifer Knapp.

Around the same time, Justin's mom had a bright idea. She wanted to share videos of his performances from Stratford Star with his grandparents and other family members who couldn't see the show in person. So she decided to create a YouTube account and post the videos online. On January 19, 2007, "kidrauhl" was born. "The next thing we knew, all these strangers were clicking onto it, probably because they recognized the song. Then it was 'Oh, he's so cute,' and then, 'Why don't you sing this song or that song?' I said [to Justin], 'Oh, they want you to sing this song—let's try,'" Pattie told *Vanity Fair*.

Over the coming weeks and months,

349,380,292 AND CLIMBING!

The total amount of views Justin's YouTube channel has received.

Pattie uploaded more...and more. "It was a horrible camera; I'm a terrible cameraman; it was awful sound, very raw video—but I put them up. Then it was 'Oh look, honey, you have a hundred views.' Then 'Oh wow, a thousand views.'... Next thing we knew, thousands and thousands of views. But it never once occurred to me that there would be a music career out of this," she continued.

It turned out that it wasn't just smitten fans the videos were attracting. Justin started getting the attention of music executives, many of whom contacted Pattie with offers of management and promises of riches. It all sounded too good to be true—and Pattie wasn't buying it.

Then came Scooter Braun. Recalling the first time he saw Justin online, he told the *Hollywood Reporter*, "I heard the tone in his voice and I saw some instrumentation and it was just raw talent. And my gut went crazy.... It was a feeling I had when I was watching. This is it. This is what I had been

> ### SAY WHAT?
>
> *"You could immediately tell that this [was] a kid who has style—he's a hip kid. It was the antithesis of Disney and Nickelodeon."*
>
> —Usher describing his first impressions of Justin, to *Vanity Fair*

Singer Justin Bieber performs at the 3rd annual Tiki Rocks The Square for the Children's Miracle Network at the Hard Rock Cafe, Times Square on September 24, 2009, in New York City.

Chapter 3:
STRATFORD STAR(T)

looking for. And then I became completely obsessed with tracking him down."

Finding Pattie was one thing. Winning her over was something different altogether. After a lot of persistence, he finally convinced her to meet him halfway; she and Justin would fly out to Atlanta to meet with him, but with no strings attached. By the end of the visit, Pattie knew they had found their man.

As it turned out, Scooter and Justin were a match made in heaven. The manager had a brilliant plan to build the singer's platform. He had raised his platform so much with YouTube already, and they worked together to continue building that fan base. He started to take the kid around to meet with local radio DJs and executives.

Soon, Justin was a hot property. Both Justin Timberlake and Usher wanted to sign him. In young Justin, Usher—who signed his own first record deal at age 14—saw a little bit of himself. Taking Justin under his wing, he had a new protégé.

HAIR APPARENT

Ever wonder what Justin would look like with a crew cut? Check out some of his old YouTube videos such as "Justin Singing 'Because of You'" for a hair-raising sight!

HONOR ROLL

One of the greatest distinctions that Stratford offers is its prestigious bronze star. Akin to the famed Hollywood Walk of Fame, each honoree is awarded with a bronze star that is placed into the sidewalks around Stratford's historical downtown and recognizes contributions to the culture and city of Stratford. Among the honorees are world-famous pianist Glenn Gould, who was a regular performer in Stratford; renowned theater and film actor Sir Alec Guinness, who performed in the inaugural Stratford Shakespeare Festival; two-time Stanley Cup champion and Stratford native Tim Taylor; and first Canadian female physician Jennie Trout.

On Canada Day, July 1, 2011, Justin Bieber was awarded his own bronze Star for his achievements in the world of music and entertainment.

Justin Bieber (r) talks with his manager before meeting with band camp students at Seminole High School in Sanford, Florida, on August 5, 2010.

Singer Justin Bieber accepts the Choice Male Artist award onstage during the 2011 Teen Choice Awards held at the Gibson Amphitheatre on August 7, 2011, in Universal City, California.

KIDRAUHL SHUFFLE

Can you arrange these YouTube videos in the order they were uploaded? Put them in order from the oldest to the most recent.

A. "Snippet of Justin on Someone's Old Drums"

B. "Justin Singing in the Bathroom – Back at One"

C. "Justin Playing Kate's Song on the Piano"

D. "Justin Singing 'Set a Place at Your Table'"

E. "Justin Singing 'So Sick' by Ne-Yo"

F. "Justin Bieber Playing the Djembe"

Answers:

1-E: Justin's first-ever upload, it was a triumph at Stratford Star and beyond!

2-A: It was the first time on YouTube that Justin strutted his stuff on the drums. It would be the first of many instruments he would rock on video.

3-C: Kidrauhl was still all about the family. Here he plays his grandmother's own composition on the keyboard.

4-B: As the demand for more videos grew, Justin and Pattie started trying out some of their favorites—and fan's requests.

5-F: Justin masters yet another instrument, the African drum the djembe.

6-D: Justin's first recorded single, this song was recorded to benefit a local Stratford charity.

Chapter 4:

WE ARE FAMILY

Chapter 4:
WE ARE FAMILY

Life in the fast lane certainly has its pitfalls. And early stardom is especially tricky to adjust to. For many young celebrities, fame can mean easy access to drugs, alcohol, and other dangerous influences. In today's gossip-magazine culture, the examples aren't difficult to find—they're everywhere.

Bieber's mentor Usher, who knows a thing or two about resisting fame's temptations as a young man, has a pragmatic view. "The pitfalls of fame come in time... [but Justin's career] should be a long story, which is what we hope for. We hope for longevity," he told CNN.

It's a credit to Justin that he's been able to navigate the muddy waters of teenage superstardom. Those who know Justin, however, understand how he keeps it together. It's about his faith, but more important, it's about the people with whom he surrounds himself.

In an interview with the Associated Press, he explained how his faith in God helps him keep perspective. "Hollywood is...a scary place. There's a lot going on, there's a lot of bad things, but there [are] also a lot of good things. I'm able to live my dream. I'm able to do a lot of good things.... I believe I have a relationship [with God] and I'm able to talk to him. And really, that's the reason I'm here, so I have to remember that. As soon as I start forgetting, I've got to click back and [remind myself]...*this is why I'm here.*"

Pattie, long skeptical of the risky world of fame, has another strategy. "We don't have yes-men around him. I don't want him being a diva," she told *Vanity Fair.*

> ## QUOTABLE *JUSTIN*
>
> *"Until three years ago...my definition of a celebrity [was] somebody who gets to ride around in a Zamboni."*
>
> **—Justin, writing in *First Step 2 Forever*, on how his conception of fame has changed**

> ## ART IMITATING LIFE
>
> *Justin's single "Up" is all about overcoming adversity. It's an inspirational song for fans, but its lyrics also reflect the perseverance that Justin has shown in his career so far.*

Scooter Braun, Usher, and Justin Bieber backstage before Justin Bieber performs at Madison Square Garden on August 31, 2010, in New York City.

Justin Bieber and mother Pattie Mallette attends The 53rd Annual GRAMMY Awards held at Staples Center on February 13, 2011, in Los Angeles, California.

SPOTLIGHT ON...MAMA JAN

Jan Smith is nothing short of a living legend. The vocal coach, based in Atlanta, has worked with some of the recording industry's top talents. Big voices from Drake to Rob Thomas to Keyshia Cole to Monica—and, of course, Usher—flock to Mama Jan to fine-tune their most precious instruments: their voices.

A coach and vocal producer, Smith has more than two decades' worth of experience in the music industry. Her latest project? Helping Justin Bieber as his voice

matures. When considering whether she was up to the challenge, Justin wrote in his autobiography, "I'm not worried. She got Usher through it, too."

In fact, Justin's inner circle is one of the biggest reasons for his successful transition. In the midst of all of the chaos of a worldwide tour, media scrutiny, and a legion of devoted fans, his team helps provide him with a sense of normalcy in an otherwise crazy world.

"Entourage" isn't the right term; for Justin, it's more like a family. He travels, of course, with his mom, who provides both parental support *and* tough love. Think a world-famous

musician is above getting grounded? Think again.

"My mom is strict. She sets boundaries. She's very concerned [about] who I'm going out with and who's an influence in my life," he told *People* magazine. Not only does he have a curfew, but he has to be off the computer by a certain hour, too. The penalties? Because I'm traveling so much my mom takes things I really, really like—like my computer or my

>
> *TWITTER-PATED:*
>
> *"i think i understand im not living a normal life anymore...but im normal. people say all sorts of stuff but i know who i am and im grateful."*
>
> **JANUARY 18, 2011**

Chapter 4:
WE ARE FAMILY

phone," he told Oprah Winfrey.

Manager Scooter Braun is also a normal presence in his life. A former party promoter, Scooter has the right perspective on the scene and how easily people can fall into it. He shed some light on why this singer might be the exception to the spoiled-young-Hollywood rule in an interview with MTV News. "Justin doesn't study the people who made it; he studies the people who haven't. He hears all the naysayers about how he's going to disappear, so he likes to look up people who used to be the so-called Justin Biebers before him and didn't go anywhere. He wants to see *why* they didn't go anywhere. The general feeling we get is that it has nothing to do with their talent and everything to do with their personal life—like the kids [who] fall into drugs and destroy

VOCABULARY

Grounded (´graun·dəd)

Grounded can mean "mentally and emotionally stable," but it can also mean big trouble! Guess which one Justin wants to be—and which one he'd like to avoid at any cost!

their own trajectory."

Also among his trusted compatriots are vocal coach "Mama" Jan Smith, Justin's self-described "secret weapon." "She's one of the greatest people in the world," Justin wrote in his autobiography, *First Step 2 Forever*. "She's like a second mom to all of us, and she's become one of the most important people in my life." Plus, she keeps him honest. "She doesn't mess around," he continues.

In spite of all the glitz and glamour, those who surround him are determined to provide some sense of normalcy for him. He has a mandatory day off every week. The directive? *Just be a kid.*

Bodyguard Kenny Hamilton keeps a lot of those external influences from breaking through to Justin. He also helps him have fun on the road. Followers of Justin's Twitter will

JUSTIN'S FAVORITE THINGS!

JB HAS A BLACK MACBOOK AIR. EVERY JUSTIN FAN KNOWS HIS COMMITMENT TO STAYING CONNECTED ONLINE. HE'S NEVER FAR FROM HIS PHONE AND COMPUTER.

Justin and his agent, Scooter Braun, ham it up at the Dolce & Gabbana Fashion Night Out in New York in September 2011.

recognize Hamilton's name. Not only are the two constantly pranking each other; it seems like they're always involved in some kind of competition. (Tweets like "@KennyHamilton Whatever #SCOREBOARD" are a frequent sight.)

And even with a busy travel schedule, Justin still goes to school. He travels with a private tutor who keeps his academic progress on track. And, like regular kids, he doesn't always love hitting the books. But he's committed to keeping education a focus in his life.

With a support system like that, it's easy to see how Justin has found a sense of normalcy in the not-so-normal world of fame.

"People are just waiting for me to personally mess up. But I'm just a regular person," Justin told *Vanity Fair*. "I'm going to make mistakes—everybody makes them. I don't think I'm perfect, by any means. But I've got such a great family, such great people surrounding me, that I know I'm not going to make a life-changing bad decision, as some people have. I've seen it happen too many

SAY WHAT?

"If he can stay on track, he will likely be that artist of our lifetime."

—*"Mama" Jan Smith on the importance of Justin staying the course*

WHO SAID WHAT?

A: "It's hard for him to be a kid. He's not a 'normal' kid. He's been really gracious with all the pressure."

B: "You can't surround yourself with people who always [tell you yes] because you start believing that stuff."

C: "[Having a normal life is] definitely a balancing act."

Answers: A–Scooter Braun; B–Justin Bieber; C–Pattie Mallette

Singers Sean Kingston and Justin Bieber attend the 2011 Teen Choice Awards at Gibson Universal Amphitheatre on August 7, 2011, in Universal City, California.

Kenny Hamilton and Justin Bieber arrive at the 'Megamind' Los Angeles Premiere at Mann Chinese 6 on October 30, 2010, in Los Angeles, California.

MEET THE INNER CIRCLE

SCOOTER BRAUN: Braun is credited with "discovering" Justin. But the manager and singer are more than just business associates; they're close friends.

PATTIE MALLETTE:  Justin's mom is a constant presence on the Biebs' tour.

KENNY HAMILTON: Justin's bodyguard keeps security tight, but he's also known to clown around with the singer.

JAN SMITH: The voice coach is a second mother to Justin and his crew.

JEREMY BIEBER:  Justin's dad doesn't come on tour with the rest of the bunch, but the two maintain a close relationship.

JAZMYN AND JAXON BIEBER:  Justin's half-siblings, he's constantly shouting out to them on Twitter when he can't spend time with them.

RYAN GOOD: Justin's stylist, "swagger coach," and confidante.

DAN KANTER:  Justin's guitarist and musical director, he's also a good friend.

SELENA GOMEZ: Justin's famous girlfriend knows a thing or two about taking celebrity in stride.

JADEN SMITH:  Growing up with famous parents gives pal Jaden a unique perspective on living life in the spotlight.

USHER:  Friend, mentor, and sounding board, Usher has remained a constant source of guidance for Justin throughout his young career.

Chapter 5:

JUST A KID

Chapter 5:
JUST A KID

He's traveled the world. He's sold millions of records. He's a best-selling author. He's been on the covers of several magazines. He's comfortable on stage, in the studio lights, and on the red carpet. He hob-nobs with celebrities all the time. He's adored by admirers the world over—young and old, male and female.

Not to mention he has more than 12 million Twitter followers and 35 million people who "Like" him on Facebook.

Just your everyday, average teenager, right? Far

TWITTER-PATED:

ok time to go to school. so excited. school is amazing. love doing math and reading. nothing is better. nothing. NOT!

JANUARY 31, 2011

2011 interview with Ellen DeGeneres, Justin made his case. "When people say I'm not normal it's wrong because I'm as normal as it gets.... I hang out with my friends. I go to the movies."

The singer has said that the hardest thing about his job is being on the road full-time. "I miss hanging out with my friends at school but having this opportunity is so great, it's a once-in-a-lifetime opportunity, it's definitely worth it."

For all of the perks of being a celebrity, he still enjoys the same things kids his age do. For his 16th birthday party, he could have had an all-star Hollywood affair. Instead, he took the time off to spend time with friends and family. There was basketball, swimming, karaoke, and even sumo wrestling. "I guess it's not as extravagant as you might think from a recording artist," he writes in *First Step 2 Forever*, "but at the end of the day, I'm still a regular kid. I don't expect, nor do I want, to be treated any differently." For his 17th birthday, he went even smaller—celebrating with family and main squeeze Selena Gomez.

15

The number of hours of schooling Justin gets in a typical week.

from it. But deep down, he's still a normal kid living a very, very abnormal life. In a

Justin Bieber (C) seen during a soccer game on the streets of Stratford on June 3, 2011, in Stratford, Canada.

Justin Bieber visits Ray's Pizza on
September 8, 2011, in New York City.

WORD SCRAMBLE

Unscramble the letters below to read the secret message.

STUNJI SKILE OT "SHLOCO" ELOPPE NI BLABKLATES

Answer: JUSTIN LIKES TO "SCHOOL" PEOPLE IN BASKETBALL.

Whenever possible, he tries to catch up with his friends. His best friends from Stratford are Ryan Butler and Chaz Somers, both of whom are familiar faces to the Bieber faithful. Former hockey teammates and close pals, the three try to keep in contact through texts, video chats, and email. They also try to take time out for each other whenever possible—which often means traveling. Justin gets to catch up with his buds each time he returns home to Stratford. And they have visited him at concerts, during off-days, and once even surprised the singer during an appearance on MTV!

Not surprisingly, the friends like to do normal stuff on the rare occasions when

ART IMITATING LIFE

Basketball is one of Justin's favorite sports. Perhaps that's why one of his first-ever performances was a cover of Lil Bow Wow's "Basketball."

Chapter 5:
JUST A KID

they see each other, whether it's shootng hoops, skateboarding, playing video games, or just hanging out. Of course, being the friend of a mega-celebrity has its perks, too. Justin has introduced his Stratford friends to some other big-name recording artists, including Eminem.

Unfortunately, the friends don't get to chill as much as they'd like. Being on the road as much as he is, waking up in a different city or even different time zone from the day before can wreak havoc on a routine. But Justin tries to keep to a schedule as best he can.

His day starts much like many people's: with school. Justin's tutor travels with him wherever he goes. He's committed to his goal to go to college one day. One of the advantages of having a tutor while traveling: he gets to learn history of the places

JUSTIN'S FAVORITE THINGS!

NBA 2K IS AMONG JUSTIN'S FAVORITE VIDEO GAMES.

he visits while he's there.

Predictably, he likes school about as much as most students do. Sometimes he just wants to "throw erasers at the teacher's head." And maybe he likes to play the occasional prank on his tutor, Jenny, too—although he tries to keep the schoolwork balanced with the merrymaking. In one funny moment in his autobiography, he writes about how he tricked his tutor with a "science experiment," which ended up with her getting a handful of butter. "Pranks vs school = pranks win all day. Can you blame me?" he writes in *First Step 2 Forever*.

But while school sometimes feels like a chore, he doesn't need to be reminded about the value of education. In fact, one of the causes closest to his heart is Pencils of Promise, an organization that helps to build schools in

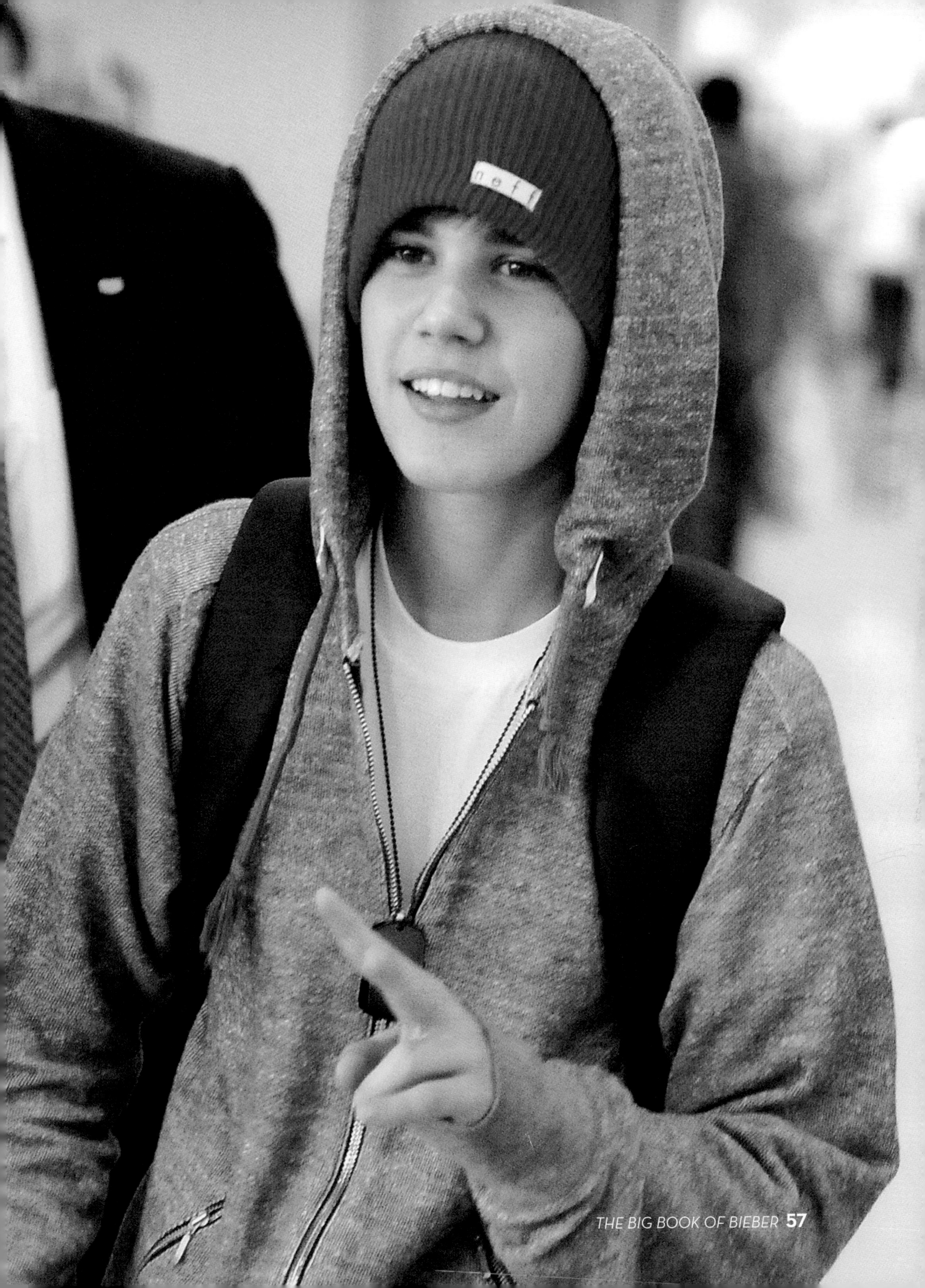
neff

Chapter 5:
JUST A KID

underdeveloped countries. The charity's mission is to provide education for those among the 75 million children worldwide who do not have access to schooling.

And let's not forget what makes him the most typical teenage boy of all. Girls!

So what kind of girl *does* Justin like?

"I like girls who are outgoing and funny, someone who's smart that I can have a good conversation with," the singer has said. "I don't like girls who wear lots of makeup and you can't see their face. Some girls are beautiful but insecure and look much better without the makeup, but decide to put loads on. I like girls with nice eyes and a nice smile."

So maybe he is a average, everyday typical teenage boy after all...

> **TRUE /** *NOT TRUE?*
>
> *Justin said the worst part about not going to a regular school is that he doesn't get to go to prom.*
>
> False, it's not getting to spend time with his friends. Besides, the singer's already had plenty of prom invitations from fans around the world!

F-F-F-FASHION!

One thing Justin and his pal do when they let loose is really silly: dressing up in costumes. Justin Tweeted this photo of himself and Ryan posing as Harry Potter and Ozzy Osbourne. Too funny!

Remember the Best Buy commercial from the Super Bowl? Justin appeared—this time with the real Ozzy Osbourne—and dressed up as a much older version of himself. (Kinda scary!)

Justin has also worn disguises out in public; he went incognito in glasses and a fake mustache at the 2011 Critics' Choice Awards. He once even wore a women's blonde wig on stage at a concert!

Justin Bieber donates a signed skateboard from his new music video to The Hard Rock Cafe. Hollywood on November 17, 2009, in Universal City, California.

An excited Justin shakes hands with Dwight Howard at the 2011 NBA All-Star Game.

WORD SEARCH

Friends, school, and fun... There are a lot of words that describe Justin's life when he's not on stage. See if you can find all of the words hidden in the puzzle below. They might be forward, backward, diagonal, across, or up and down.

BASKETBALL
CHAZ

CHRISTIAN
DOWNTIME
FRIENDS
HANGING OUT

HOMEWORK
MOVIES
RYAN
RELAX
SKATEBOARDING

```
B O D N G I M K E N O F U S N A
S J C N I O D M A C I Z P K B L
M I H A N G I N G O U T Z A N O
Q T A I C T U F W X W I S T A T
H O Z S N E T S P O H K R E W P
T A N W U O D E T R E I E B E E
E I O T H N I N E T O T S O I G
C D T U E P R A B R I E C A R V
N R O I T U I A T N M R E R T H
B U R S X A L E R A D E T D D A
T F E S A L R N G Y A O B I C V
U E O Y G E T O P R R D O N A E
N I K R O W E M O H G H Y G D Q
A R I R P D R A C E B I M F A Y
R P N A I T S I R H C H W E S M
C M O V I E S S T U B E A Y H E
```

Chapter 6

JUSTIN THE COMEDIAN

Chapter 6:
JUSTIN THE COMEDIAN

Further proof that Justin isn't all work and no play: he finds plenty of time to clown around. Readers of his Twitter page know it all too well. Among the serious messages he posts to his Twitter feed—from updates about music and appearances to inspirational messages to fans—he's also quick with a joke. One of his favorites? Chuck Norris.

The Web site ChuckNorrisFacts.com first popularized jokes about the mustachioed action star, painting him as the uber tough guy. The site, a viral success in 2010, encourages visitors to contribute their own "facts" about the actor.

"RANDOM CHUCK NORRIS MOMENT – CHUCK NORRIS doesnt need a Twitter...he is already following you," Justin tweeted.

In 2010, Justin helmed the popular comedy Web site, FunnyorDie.com, which was created by funnymen Will Ferrell and Adam McKay. As an April Fool's Day prank, Bieber "took over" the site, saying, "It's mine. I bought it. Now it's BieberorDie. Anything that's not Bieber...dies." In the hilarious clip, he extols the virtues of being Justin Bieber: "I talk loudly in libraries. I swim directly after I eat. I don't care."

Bieber starred in a number of videos for the comedy site prank including hilarious send-ups of some famous viral videos. In one clip, the camera cuts between the popular "OMG Cat" video and Justin's OMG reaction watching the video. In another, he's stunned by the dramatics of Chuck Norris wrestling a bear in a clip from *Walker, Texas Ranger*. His acting chops are also apparent. In one clip, he pretends to be fresh from a tough day at the dentist; in another, he takes a comedic tumble worthy of (quintessential physical comedian) Chevy Chase himself.

The April Fool's Day antics were only the beginning. Later that year, Justin popped up on the long-running late-night comedy show *Saturday Night Live*. Scheduled as the musical guest, Bieber made a few cameos in the show's sketches, including a hilarious bit in which he was the object of his high school teacher's affection. Proving that he could poke fun at himself and his heartthrob

---

QUOTABLE *JUSTIN*

"I want to be on TV."

—Justin, when asked as a child what he wanted to be when he grew up, as featured in Justin Bieber: Never Say Never

---

THIS DAY IN JB-ISTORY

Justin takes over comedy Web site FunnyorDie.com, renaming it "BieberorDie.com." Hilarity ensues!

APRIL 1, 2010

Chuck Norris

Comedian Dana Carvey performs at The Ice House Comedy Club on January 18, 2011 in Pasadena, California.

PRANK'D!

Beliebers, the prankster is back in action. Recently, Justin and his pals recorded a video of themselves trying out the latest prank trend: coning. (Yes, this really is a thing!) Ordering two ice cream cones from the drive thru, Justin pulls up and grabs the ice cream cones—from the top!—and then drives off, much to the bewilderment of the window attendant. Suffice it to say he made quite the mess. So maybe the joke was on himself, after all?

In the same video, he also tries to exchange a Frosty (a well-known milkshake from Wendy's) at a Burger King drive thru. Talk about getting creamed!

image, Bieber winked and tossed his hair at the smitten teacher, played by Tina Fey, throughout the sketch.

He returned to *SNL* in 2011 to join guest host Dana Carvey in two very funny sketches. The first, a revival of Carvey's beloved "Church Chat," saw Justin leading the Church Lady herself into temptation. In a fake movie trailer

sending up *Single White Female*–esque movies like the then-new-release *The Roommate*, Justin stars as a college student who just might be the object of his creepy roommate's obsession. "This isn't going to be one of those things where our friendship starts out fine but then you get really possessive and crazy because I'm not really up for

TWITTER-PATED:

"*RANDOM CHUCK NORRIS MOMENT: The reason it rains is CHUCK NORRIS scared the clouds, and they wet themselves. #fact*"

JANUARY 27, 2011

that," Justin tells Andy Samberg in the clip. He has also showed up on *The Late Show with David Letterman*, reading one of the host's trademark top 10 lists. Among the top 10 "Little Known Facts About Justin Bieber," the musician again makes fun of his own image, sharing "facts," such as, "As hard as I try I don't know how to not be adorable" and "Last week I accidentally waited in line for two hours for my own autograph."

In February 2011 he took over the world of news-comedy, sitting in for Jon Stewart on *The Daily Show*. In a spoof of body-swapping movies like *Freaky Friday* and *Vice Versa*, the two pretend to be trapped in the other's bodies. Bieber, playing Jon Stewart, agrees to switch back bodies, but not before he fondles his own hair one last time. "It's just so natural. It's just so pure," he jokes.

Probably his most frequent comedy foil, however, is late-night talk-show host Jimmy Fallon. Bieber has

appeared on the show several times, and each time the two have produced comedy gold. In a recent spoof of Bieber's television commercial for the fragrance Someday, Fallon enters the scene as an "older, fatter" version of the Biebs. "What happened?" Bieber asks. "You just got busy. And your metabolism changed a bit," Fallon responds.

"I can eat like five slices of pizza and I don't gain an ounce," the incredulous singer says. "Well, enjoy it, dude," Fallon admonishes.

Fallon also has a popular video series called "Reflections with Justin Bieber," in which he parodies the musician's charmed life.

Justin has hinted in the past that he would like to star in a movie someday. Recently, the Hollywood casting rumors

---

SAY WHAT?

"I have to say, seeing you in person is affecting me in a way I didn't think it quite would."

."—Dana Carvey as the Church Lady, to Justin Bieber on Saturday Night Live

---

HAIR APPARENT

The Justin Bieber 'do has become so popular, that it's not just SNL celebrities trying the wig on for size. A popular costume craze, the Bieber wig is available from multiple retailers trying to cash in on the singer's signature coif.

Actor/Comedian Jon Stewart speaks onstage during 'ReAct Now: Music & Relief' at the MTV Times Square Studios September 10, 2005, in New York City.

have been swirling. Some say he is in talks to star in a forthcoming Ashton Kutcher movie. Many have already named Justin the heir apparent to Kutcher, whose former show *Punk'd* is getting a reboot on MTV. Knowing the Biebs is a notorious prankster, he'd certainly make a good host for the show. He's slated to appear on the new version's season premiere—pranking fellow musician and friend Taylor Swift. But he won't take on permanent hosting duties on the series.

With his natural on-screen charisma and indisputable sense of humor, Bieber could be bound for silver-screen stardom. After all, he's already broken the bank at theatres with his concert documentary *Justin Bieber: Never Say Never*. But don't count the singer as a Hollywood actor just yet. He is—and always will be—a musician first.

ART IMITATING LIFE

"No one really cares for 'funny' anymore anyway. I mean, try to define funny and then try to define Bieber, and you will understand completely."

—Justin, in a statement about rebranding FunnyorDie.com as BieberorDie.com

F-F-F-FASHION!

Tons of people have tried on Justin's style for size. The Bieber was one of 2010's most popular Halloween costumes. So what is Justin's signature style? Well, it has a lot of people seeing purple.

In many ways, he dresses like your average teenage boy—but in a hip-hop world. There are the hoodies, the ballcaps, and the stylin' sneakers. There's also every celebrity's favorite accessory: the sunglasses. Bieber has rocked some purple Ray Ban–style frames in the past. That look was the model for the 3-D glasses for his release of *Justin Bieber: Never Say Never*.

His own take on his personal style is simpler: "This is me. I wear a hoodie. I'm just easy," Justin told Chris Connelly of *Nightline*.

Taylor Swift and Justin Bieber attend Z100's Jingle Ball 2009 presented by H&M at Madison Square Garden on December 11, 2009, in New York City.

Justin Bieber performs
supporting Taylor Swift at MEN
Arena on November 24, 2009, in
Manchester, England.

DOUBLE TAKE

Being Justin Bieber must be lots of fun. Plenty of people in Hollywood have spoofed the young star, dressing up as the singer himself. Have you seen all these stars in disguise?

Miley Cyrus– Spoofing the star on *Saturday Night Live*, Miley gets Justin's signature wink down to a *T*!

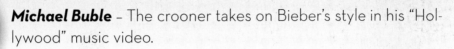

Michael Buble – The crooner takes on Bieber's style in his "Hollywood" music video.

Josh Duhamel – The *Transformers* actor looks slick at the 2011 Kids' Choice Awards.

Jon Stewart on *The Daily Show with Jon Stewart* – The talk-show host goes green with hair envy.

Jimmy Fallon on *Late Night with Jimmy Fallon* – Winking at Justin's new perfume commercial: "Someday you'll look like this." The talk show host has dressed as Bieber in several videos and on-air skits.

Pauly D – The *Jersey Shore* star dressed as the Biebs for a Halloween DJ appearance in Las Vegas.

Mike Greenberg, cohost of New York radio show "Mike and Mike in the Morning" – Greenberg lost a bet but gained a new hairstyle.

Chapter 7
MUSICAL INFLUENCES

Chapter 7:
MUSICAL INFLUENCES

"I've been a musician my whole life," Bieber told Ellen DeGeneres in a 2011 interview. Viewers of *Justin Bieber: Never Say Never*—and really, any casual scholar of the singer—knows this much to be true.

From the very beginning, there was always music—whether it was on the radio or the friends and family who assembled to raise their own voices in chorus. There is little doubt that the seeming ever-presence of music in his life has influenced Bieber's artistry.

From his earliest days as a performer, his song selection alone showed his musical education. As comfortable with Sarah McLachlan as Stevie Wonder, his interests ranged far and wide. You can hear it in his performances. He delivered his Stratford Star performance of "Respect" with a confidence worthy of the Queen of Soul herself. His rendition of Edwin McCain's heartbreak anthem "I'll Be" was imbued with a sadness the then-12-year-old couldn't possibly have experienced personally.

> **QUOTABLE** *JUSTIN*
>
> *"He's everyone's inspiration. Whether you're a country artist or a rapper, most people look at Michael Jackson as one of their top inspirations."*
>
> **—Justin to ABC News in the days after Jackson's death**

One thing is clear: Justin is no mimic. "I've never tried to sound like anybody," he told *McLean's* magazine. He's said that the worst thing he could hear about himself is to be described as a carbon copy of somebody else. Even as a youngster, he possessed the most precious vocal gift a singer could have: the ability to infuse emotion into song.

His vast musical education started at home with his mom. Between the pop songs of the day they heard played on the radio and the contemporary Christian music they heard from the praise band at their church on Sundays, there were a lot of different sounds at work.

"By the time I was four or five, I could climb up on the stool and play the [drum] kit all by myself, and, about that same time, I discovered I could get up on the piano bench and pound on that, too," he writes in *First Step 2 Forever*. "Much to everyone's surprise, it started sounding like actual music."

Jeremy Bieber picked up on his son's love of music, too, and shared his love of rock 'n' roll with his son. Soon Justin

> **DID YOU KNOW?**
>
> *Justin's song "Pray" was inspired by Michael Jackson's 1987 hit "Man in the Mirror."*

Edwin McCain performs at the NASCAR Hall of Fame Reception and Dinner on May 18, 2011, in Charlotte, North Carolina.

Justin Bieber and members of Boyz II Men perform at Madison Square Garden on August 31, 2010, in New York City.

SPOTLIGHT ON BOYZ II MEN

Boyz II Men may well have been the most successful R&B group of the 1990s. The clean-cut quartet from Philadelphia had a stranglehold on the charts with their so-called "New Jack Swing" and "hip-hop doo-wop."

Their rise to fame happened seemingly overnight (a trajectory quite similar to Justin's own). The group formed in 1988 at the High School of the Performing Arts in Philadelphia, Pennsylvania. A year later, they snuck backstage at a Bell Biv Devoe concert and gave an impromptu audition to Michael Bivins, singing a version of "Can You Stand the Rain" by Bivins' former group, New Edition. Suitably impressed, Bivins offered them a deal on the spot.

Just one year later, *Cooleyhighharmony* was released and Wanya Morris, Shawn Stockman, Michael McCary, and Nathan Morris were atop the charts. A long string of successes would follow, including multiple Grammys.

Known for their intricate four-part harmonies and clean-cut image, they produced a string of smash hits in the 1990s, including "Motownphilly," "The End of the Road," "It's So Hard to Say Goodbye to Yesterday," and "On Bended Knee," the last of which they performed onstage with superfan Justin in 2010.

was strumming chords from Bob Dylan's "Knockin' on Heaven's Door" with his dad. A whole new avenue of music opened up. After Dylan came the full-throttle guitars of Jimi Hendrix, Aerosmith, and Van Halen. "To play metal or even the 1980s hair band stuff like Journey and Twisted Sister, you've gotta know the so-called power chords, and Dad taught me a few tricks there, too," Justin wrote in his memoir. He was well on his way to becoming a bona fide guitarist.

There are plenty of bands who have influenced Justin's sound, but perhaps none have influenced

SAY WHAT?

"Justin Bieber could be like Prince. Justin Bieber could be like Michael Jackson where his career is...so long."

—will.i.am speculating on Bieber's longevity as an artist to Radio Disney

Chapter 7:
MUSICAL INFLUENCES

him more vocally than Boyz II Men. The quartet, known for their a capella harmonies and polished performance skills, were a radio staple in the 1990s.

Justin has certainly also taken plenty of cues from Michael Jackson, who he cites as his all-time greatest influence. "Michael [Jackson] was able to reach audiences from young to old; he never limited himself. He was so broad, everybody loved him, and that's what my goal is—to basically make people happy, to inspire them, and to have everyone root for me," Justin told *Vanity Fair*.

And certainly, there are parallels between the two artists. Jackson's recording career began at an early age, too. Along with his siblings as the group the Jackson Five, he recorded his first record at age 10. Navigating worldwide fame is no easy feat, but he was able to translate his success as a child star into unparalleled success as an adult performer.

Jackson was more than just a singer. He was an all-around performer. Known as "the King of Pop," he is celebrated as much for his talent as a dancer as he is for his incredible music. As a solo artist, Jackson's pedigree is formidable and likely will never be eclipsed. He is one of the best-selling artists of all time, with more than 10 Grammys to his credit.

"He was just an all-around entertainer. He wasn't a singer. He wasn't a dancer.... He explored so many avenues. He did it all," Justin told ABC News.

Justin looks back to classic artists for musical inspiration, but he has his other foot in the world of contemporary pop and R&B, as well. Mentor Usher is among the artists who inform his sound—and stage performance.

Ask him who else influences him, and the answers will change daily. He thinks the Beatles, Jackson, and Tupac are among the best ever. He also cites Prince and Ozzy Osbourne—two very different performers both known for their outsized stage presence—as influences. Bieber also likes fellow chart-toppers Rihanna, Lil Wayne, Drake, Chris Brown, and Sean Kingston. (Brown and Kingston are friends and

> ## THIS DAY IN JB-ISTORY
>
> *Justin's first Grammy Awards appearance (of hopefully many, many more). He was nominated as Best New Artist and also performed with Usher and Jaden Smith.*
>
> **FEBRUARY 13, 2011**

> ## UNDER THE INFLUENCE
>
> *From Aretha Franklin to Usher, many artists have influenced Justin. But the first song he ever performed publicly was Matchbox 20's "3 A.M."*

Justin Bieber and Usher perform onstage
during The 53rd Annual GRAMMY Awards
held at Staples Center on February 13,
2011, in Los Angeles, California.

Chapter 7:
MUSICAL INFLUENCES

collaborators.) And Kanye West—who recently worked with Justin to produce a remix of Bieber's "Runaway Love" featuring Raekwon of the Wu Tang Clan—is also a fave.

He's also a big fan—and friend—of multiplatinum singer-songwriter Taylor Swift. Former tour mates, the singers have been friends for years and keep up with each other via Twitter, since the two—with their own busy schedules—are very rarely in the same

TWITTER-PATED:

"You think you've heard LOUD screaming in your life.. Then @justinbieber comes out and does a surprise song during your show. Woah. Unreal."

—TAYLOR SWIFT, VIA TWITTER, AFTER JUSTIN SURPRISED FANS AT HER AUGUST 24, 2011, CONCERT

place at the same time!

Recently, Bieber surprised Swift fans by showing up to her August 24, 2011, concert at the Staples Center. In a break between songs, the band started playing "Baby." Taylor paused to ask, "Do you guys want to see my friend Justin?" He joined the stage and the two performed a duet of his smash hit—to the amazement of Swift's shocked audience!

JUSTIN BIEBER: STYLE ICON

It's evident that Justin has taken plenty of Michael Jackson's examples to heart. His dancing, singing, and timeless music has all had a profound effect on Justin's musical philosophy. But don't forget style. Justin's on-stage attire on the My World Tour looks very familiar indeed.

Pop singer Michael Jackson in a still from the video for his hit single 'Thriller' which was released on December 2, 1983, in Los Angeles, California.

Justin Bieber performs at Nokia Theatre L.A. Live on July 20, 2010, in Los Angeles, California.

MEET THE INFLUENCES

Michael Jackson: The powerful voice, the superhuman dance moves, and the universal appeal of his music makes Jackson an impressive role model. Justin also admires Jackson for his lifelong commitment to philanthropy.

Usher: Justin can learn a lot from Usher, who has been a recording artist since his teens. He can also learn a mean dance move or two.

The Beatles: The top-selling musical artists of all time, the Beatles pushed the very boundaries of what music could be. Justin calls them among "the best."

Prince: Another all-around entertainer, Prince's songs are as fresh today as they were decades ago. You think Justin has a fondness for purple because of this guy?

Bob Dylan: Known for his lyrics as much as his music, Justin can appreciate Dylan's commitment to songwriting as a craft.

Beyonce: Okay, he might have a little crush on her. But Beyonce is an undisputed success as a performer—something Justin has taken strides to accomplish himself.

Chapter 8:

JUSTIN CONQUERS THE INTERNET

Chapter 8:
JUSTIN CONQUERS THE INTERNET

When Justin was born in 1994, the Internet was, like the singer, still in its infancy. In fact, only one out of four homes in America even had a computer. As if that's not shocking enough, only 2 *percent* of households had Internet access!

The expansion of the Internet and its capabilities increased dramatically in the next decade. Americans were going online for everything from shopping to researching to communicating. The worldwide web was more than just a place to visit. It was a place to communicate.

One thing's for sure: Justin's career as a musician owes a lot to the Internet. When Pattie posted those first YouTube videos of Justin singing at the Stratford Star, Justin became more than just a local singer. People from all over the world were watching. As the number of hits started to climb, his audience grew and grew.

And as Justin's videos began to gain popularity, he began to get the attention of people within the music industry. Enter Scooter Braun. The music promoter knew a good thing when he saw it. He also understood the power of the Internet in building a platform. Before Justin, the careers of young musicians followed a predictable pattern. It was difficult for an artist to emerge without a traditional platform. The typical springboard was television, and most of the young stars to emerge in the '90s—singers like Miley Cyrus and the Jonas Brothers—were supported by their shows on children's cable networks such as the Disney Channel or Nickelodeon. "Every label turned me down saying, 'Justin doesn't have a show on Disney or Nickelodeon. He will not work.' I said, 'You guys don't get it. I have a platform that's more connected because all the stats show kids spend all their time on the Internet,'" manager Scooter Braun told Chris Connelly of ABC News.

Braun was right. The response to Justin's music was massive. It was obvious he was breaking the mold. Once Justin and Pattie agreed to sign on with Scooter, the manager didn't angle for a television vehicle. Instead, he put together a plan to increase Justin's

$12 MILLION

The amount of people following @justinbieber on Twitter. The singer broke the 12 million–subscriber threshold in August 2011.

SAY WHAT?

"He had 'it.'... The definition of 'viral' is what's happened."

—Scooter Braun to Nightline

Singer Justin Bieber speaks on-stage during the 2011 MTV Video Music Awards at Nokia Theatre L.A. Live on August 28, 2011, in Los Angeles, California.

Justin Bieber speaks onstage during the BET Awards '11 held at the Shrine Auditorium on June 26, 2011, in Los Angeles, California.

WORD SCRAMBLE

Unscramble the letters below to read the secret message.

SITJUN
WALSAY TYSAS
"DONCENCET" OT
SHI SNAF

Answers: JUSTIN AL-
WAYS STAYS "CONNECT-
ED," TO HIS FANS.

Internet presence even further. It was a decision that saw immediate returns, making him one of the Internet's first homegrown stars.

Part of what fans responded to in Justin was his accessibility. He communicated directly with fans on YouTube and, later, Twitter. He read and responded to his fan mail. He was no Hollywood-created confection; he was a real person with real dreams and aspirations.

The efforts helped humanize Justin to a fan base that couldn't ordinarily have interaction with other artists. It was a move that eventually got the attention of record companies and producers. Looking back, there is little doubt that the

> ### QUOTABLE JUSTIN
> *"It's good to keep fans in the loop."*
> **—Bieber to ABC News/Nightline**

Chapter 8:
JUSTIN CONQUERS THE INTERNET

unconventional marketing strategy helped the musician to land his record deal.

Today he is one of the most searched people on the Internet. His albums and singles have consistently charted among iTunes' top downloads. Small wonder, then, that he was named one of *Time* magazine's 100 Most Influential People of the Year. He was also 2010's Most influential Twitter Celebrity by *Forbes* magazine, besting even rival recording artist Lady Gaga (and her legion of more than 13 million Twitter followers).

He has used the Internet as a way to keep fans around the world on the cutting edge of all things Biebs, announcing everything from appearances to new projects to inspirational messages for his fans. It's his way to make every fan feel like he or she is an insider.

In anticipation of the release of *My World* 2.0, Justin kept his followers in the loop by tweeting updates on the album release on a nearly daily basis. The marketing efforts worked. *My World* 2.0 sold more than 1 million copies in presale—that

is, *before* the CD was even in stores.

Music videos, once strictly the province of music-television networks like MTV, are another huge Internet draw for Bieber. His videos are among the tops on streaming sites like Vevo and download sites such as iTunes.

He has also used Twitter and his Web site, among other avenues, to generate attention to the many charitable causes close to his heart. In the aftermath of the Japanese earthquakes, many celebrities took to the Internet to rally support for the many victims of the tragedy. Bieber encouraged his own fans to donate to the Red Cross' relief efforts. He has also raised awareness and generated donations for Pencils of Promise, an organization with which he is directly involved that helps further worldwide education.

In perhaps the most staggering moment of Internet kismet, Justin even got a hit single out of it. Kanye West, writing on his own Twitter feed, tweeted, "Listening to Justin Bieber 'Run Away Love' [sic]. I love

> ## DID YOU KNOW?
>
> One of his early YouTube posts, a cover of "With You" by Chris Brown, got more than 1 million hits in the first month!

> ## VOCABULARY
>
> ### Viral (vī • rəl)
>
> Oftentimes it's something you don't want to catch, like a cold. But when it refers to the Internet, it means a piece of information—text, audio, or video—that gains popularity quickly and exponentially.

Justin Bieber performs during the fan event at La Qua Garden amusement park on October 13, 2010, in Tokyo, Japan.

Chapter 8:
JUSTIN CONQUERS THE INTERNET

Sunday mornings in the crib... This song is the jam." Bieber caught Kanye's tweet and responded with thanks for the shout-out.

"So bugged out that me and @justinbieber are tweeting at the same time... Social networking is pretty awesome," Kanye continued. As it turned out, the chance conversation was indeed an awesome coincidence. Two weeks later,

West's remix of "Runaway Love" featuring Raekwon was completed. The single was a success for all three artists and a powerful testament to the efficacy of social networking—or, more specifically in this case, micro-blogging.

In a world of rapidly changing technology, it took a young person like Justin to harness its potential. And as the influence of technology grows, expect Jus-

> ### TWITTER-PATED:
>
> "...12 000 000 followers ...... Youu. Guys are incredible!!! Really proud to call u my #beliebers. No ones on the level that my fans r on."
>
> AUGUST 18, 2011

JUSTIN REACHES OUT

Talk about using the Internet for the greater good! Australian teenager Casey Heynes had taken to the Web to lash out at bullies who were physically and verbally tormenting him at school on a daily basis. The video caught the attention of Justin, and the singer reached out to Heynes, flying the teenager and his family to attend the star's concert in Melbourne. The video depicts Heynes fighting back against his attackers.

Bieber, who has long been vocal about stopping teenage bullying, alerted his Twitter followers to Heynes' plight: "Pretty special night tonight in MELBOURNE....surprised someone me and the team look up to. A kid with a lot of courage. 'This is Casey the punisher...a kid who stood up for himself against bullying. A real life hero."

Justin Bieber performs during his "My World Tour" concert in Manila, Philippines on Tuesday May 10, 2011.

Justin Bieber boards his tour bus after meeting with band camp students at Seminole High School in Sanford, Florida, on August 5, 2010.

TWITTER WINNERS

In 2010, Bieber dominated the Twitterverse, becoming the most influential Twitter celebrity according to a study done by Klout for *Forbes* magazine. The study not only charts how many followers each person has on his or her feed, but more important, the impact of his or her opinions. Here's the full list of the top 20 celebrities, ranging from musicians like Justin to television stars to writers and politicians.

1. Justin Bieber (@justinbieber)

2. Paulo Coelho (@paulocoelho), celebrated Brazilian novelist

3. Joe Jonas (@joejonas), eldest Jonas brother and solo musician

4. Kanye West (@kanyewest), multiplatinum recording artist and producer

5. The Dalai Lama (@DalaiLama), religious icon

6. Nick Jonas (@nickjonas), middle JoBro and solo musician

7. Lady Gaga (@ladygaga), singer, pianist, and fashionista

8. Conan O'Brien (@ConanOBrien), late-night talk show host and comedian

9. Diddy (@iamdiddy), successful music producer and rapper

10. Hayley Williams (@yelyahwilliams), lead singer of Paramore

11. Barack Obama (@BarackObama), president of the United States

12. Kim Kardashian (@KimKardashian), reality television star

13. Tyrese (@Tyrese), actor

14. Federico Devito (@federicodevito), Brazilian heartthrob

15. Jose Serra (@joseserra), Brazilian politician

16. Ellen DeGeneres (@theEllenShow), daytime talk show host

17. Angela Simmons (@AngelaSimmons), reality star, fashion maven, and daughter of Joseph Simmons

18. Katy Perry (@katyperry), pop star

19. Roger Ebert (@ebertchicago), longtime film critic

20. Rick Warren (@RickWarren), best-selling author and evangelical minister

Chapter 9:

JUSTIN: THE BOOK

Chapter 9:
JUSTIN: THE BOOK

In October 2010 HarperCollins released Justin's autobiography, *First Step 2 Forever*. The book tells Justin's life story in his own words, revealing the portrait of a very humble, self-possessed musician on the rise.

It should come as no surprise to Justin's fans that the story begins with them. The singer seems always to put his fans front and center. The book opens with a dedication to his faithful, who he calls "the greatest fans in the world." He wrote, "Every one of you is 'My Favorite Girl' for a different reason, because each of you is special in your own way. Everywhere I go, whatever I do, I try to connect with as many of you as possible."

That's not just lip service. Bieber has made a career out of his accessibility to fans. "You might just be talking to your friends on Twitter saying you have a one-in-a-million chance of reaching me and now I'm following you. My dreams used to be a one-in-a-million chance as well," he continued.

The book traces Justin's early years and childhood, providing a love letter to his hometown of Stratford. "I'm a proud Canadian and I hope that comes through in everything I do," he wrote.

He talks about the importance of family—his close relationships with his parents Pattie and Jeremy and the support system he received from his maternal grandparents. "That's how we are in my family. Every person gives what they have... Along with a lot of other blessings, I got my family—just the way they are."

He also addresses the difficulties of being a child of divorced parents. Showing a remarkable maturity, he understands the realities that contributed to his parents' split. "My mom and dad were in their late teens when I was born... My dad was basically a kid, doing his best to handle huge responsibilities. Lately, I've started to understand how hard that is."

He praises his mom for allowing him to find his calling in life and encouraging him to play music. To him, that encouragement was the one thing that fostered his emergence as a musician beyond any other

---

THIS DAY IN JB-ISTORY

Justin signs his first recording contract, with Island Def Jam Records.

APRIL 13, 2008

TWITTER-PATED: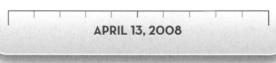

"Sometimes this is the most fun ever. Other time its really hard and theres so much pressure. Thanks 2 everyone for the support, means a lot."

APRIL 14, 2010

Fans wait to meet Justin Bieber as he signs
copies of his new book *First Step 2 Forever:
My Story* held at The Relentless Garage

WHO AM I?

- I am a big name in the music industry.
- You will soon see me on a weekly television series.
- I have worked closely with everyone from Mariah Carey to Outkast to Avril Lavigne.
- Justin writes in *First Step 2 Forever* that meeting me was "one of the most important moments in [his] life.
- I share a name with a large U.S. city.

influence. "If there's an annoying little kid in your life...who wants to make noise and pretend to play music, I hope you'll put up with him. Because, at some point, he won't be playing anymore. He'll be *playing*... How else are they supposed to learn?"

Justin recounts the last moments of his own musical obscurity. He had appeared in Stratford Star, but most of the people in his town still didn't know that he sang. Scooter Braun, who was desperate to land the

young musician as a client, had made a phone call to Justin's school, and the die was cast. Administrators discovered Justin's YouTube offerings and suddenly realized they had a celebrity in their midst. They put together a montage of YouTube clips to play during the morning announcements. "Kids had no idea I did music. They didn't hang out at the tourist places where I was busking.... When Mom finally let me talk to Scooter on the phone, I was like, "'Dude, why did you do

11 WEEKS

The consecutive number of weeks Justin Bieber: First Step 2 Forever *spent on the* New York Times *best seller list.*

Chapter 9:
JUSTIN: THE BOOK

that?... Don't you know eighth graders eat their wounded?'"

By the end of the conversation, both Scooter and Justin knew it was the beginning of a beautiful friendship. Reflecting on the connection they had in that first conversation, Justin wrote, "Sure, he was young, but he was polite and super-motivated. He knew a lot about the business. And he believed in me."

As history has proven, Scooter's instincts were right. In no time at all, Justin was signed to a record deal, climbing the charts, and embarking on a world tour across five continents. "It was crazy... Suddenly the whole world was paying attention," he wrote.

His mentor Usher offered him some sage advice as he embarked on his first world tour. "The

> **DID YOU KNOW?**
> The title of Justin's autobiography was inspired by inspirational words from Usher.

successful journey starts with the first step. And obviously that first step is the hardest. It's a lot to ask of someone so young to take on such an incredible feat. You've got to pace yourself. Enjoy yourself. Go out there and know that all this hard work has paid off, and this is the moment for you to enjoy it."

Much of Justin's book is a tour diary, which gives readers a real inside look at what it's like to be on the road. Photographs by Robert Caplin provide candid shots of life on tour and are a visual companion to Justin's words.

"Traveling has definitely opened my eyes to different cultures and the way people see things... [It] has taught me more than any school ever taught me. And I've done more geography than most students," he wrote.

JUSTIN'S FAVORITE THINGS!

PIZZA WITH PINEAPPLE
"SINGERS AREN'T SUPPOSED TO HAVE DAIRY BEFORE THE SHOW, BUT WE ALL KNOW I'M A RULE BREAKER. PIZZA IS JUST SO GOOD!"

Chapter 9:
JUSTIN: THE BOOK

In between the incredible story of his rise to fame, his overnight successes, and his jet-setting lifestyle, there are moments of humor and levity in the book. He talks about the hijinks he and his Stratford friends got into as kids, the pranks he's played on his tour mates, the drama of his first driver's test, and the real deal behind his disastrous first date.

It's a rags-to-riches story, and Justin recounts it honestly and with a great deal of humbleness. "The success I've achieved comes to me from God, through the people who love and support me, and I include my fans in that. Every single one of you lifts me a little higher."

If the aim is to inspire his fans to reach for their own dreams, Justin hits the mark perfectly. The book's closing words are Justin's own mantra and a call to arms for all dreamers: "never say never."

> ### UNDER THE INFLUENCE
> Reacting to the death of his musical idol, Justin writes "If I can do one-tenth of the good Michael Jackson did for others, I can really make a difference in this world."

MATCH-MAKING

Justin's got much love for the people who surround him. Can you match his descriptions from First Step 2 Forever *with the people to whom they belong?*

A: "An absolute sweetheart who has a vivacious, goofy personality."

B: "He gives off this great, calm, friendly vibe that just makes you glad to be there."

C: "So sweet... A cool person and a real pro."

D: "He treats life like chess, always eight moves ahead."

Answers: A-Pattie Mallette, B-Usher, C-Taylor Swift, D-Scooter Braun

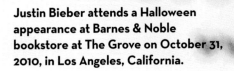

BIEBER

Justin Bieber attends a Halloween appearance at Barnes & Noble bookstore at The Grove on October 31, 2010, in Los Angeles, California.

A fan holds a book by Justin Bieber ahead of the European movie premiere of *Never Say Never* at the o2 arena in London on February 16, 2011.

THE FANS SPEAK!

"This book is a fabulous inspiration to those who are striving to pursue a difficult career, but above all, it's a way people can understand Bieber and where he comes from. It's a beautiful story that is written in a conversational way suitable for teens and above."

"'If you feel like a freak because you don't have a normal family, I've got news for you: pretty much nobody does,' [Bieber] writes in one moving chapter about his own family. In one sentence, he says pretty much what took Jonathan Franzen 576 pages to say in *The Corrections*."

"I thought the book was great. Being a 16 year old that is OBSESSED with Justin Bieber and all. Even if you're not a fan of him, I can guarantee you will enjoy the book. Reading it will probably give you more respect for him. It tells you EVERYTHING about his life that you would want to know."

"It was a gr8 book I LOVED it! I think any GIRL should READ it NOW!!!!"

"In his very first book, Bieber fills in his fans on how a lot can change in three years.... Never-before-seen pics of Beiber on and off stage and his private moments that make this a must-have."

"Oh my gosh, i am a huge fan of Justin Bieber so OF COURSE i bought this book. I read the whole thing in less than 2 days and it's so AWESOME!!!!!!!!!!!!!!! I'm about to read it again and then again and again and again cuz this book is awesome. Justin Bieber rocks the book rocks and EVERY belieber should have this. Even not beliebers should have this. I luv JB!!!!"

"JB's book, like his music, is rife with allusion and difficult challenges, it takes a genius of his caliber to challenge the established order and force people to examine their lives and core values. There is too much anti-war sentiment and not enough really awesome hairdos in our culture. We need real art to bond us in times of material excess in the midst of financial crisis, we need energetic teenagers to show us the real power of marketing and how embracing our cultural roots can put us back on the map as the supreme world power, after all, we made the maps, why should our place be in jeopardy? If this book proves anything, it proves that cynicism is dead."

Chapter 10:

JUSTIN:
THE MOVIE

Chapter 10:
JUSTIN: THE MOVIE

*J*ustin Bieber: Never Say Never premiered just weeks before the singer's 17th birthday. Opening in the usually quiet month of February, the typical box-office doldrums, the movie was a runaway success. According to the authoritative Web site BoxOfficeMojo.com, the film is the third-highest-grossing documentary film ever released.

Far from being a typical concert documentary like some of its recent predecessors—including Miley Cyrus and the Jonas Brothers' 3-D offerings—Justin's film sets out to tell the full story of the artist and his musical education.

Reflecting on Justin's childhood, grandfather Bruce Dale says in the movie, "Pattie's friends were musical and they encouraged Justin." When her friends recognized his budding talent as a percussionist, they held a local benefit to raise funds for a proper drum set. Justin wowed the crowed with some quite complicated jazz drumming—a rare feat for an eight-year-old—and the family came home with enough money to buy a bona fide drum kit. "He'd go into the furnace

$73 MILLION

The gross U.S. box office receipts for Justin Bieber: Never Say Never.

room and he would bang those drums like you wouldn't believe. And the worst part of it was, he was good," Dale continued.

When he began singing, even his friends didn't know about his hidden talent. "I was like, whoa, where did this come from man?" said friend Ryan Butler.

Record executives were at first skeptical of the singer's untraditional platform. He didn't have a television platform, but rather a homegrown based built on Internet views. But he quickly won the skeptics over. "My first impression was, *Wow, the Macaulay Culkin of music.* He came in and he soaked up all the air in the room and he [sang] really well. But it wasn't even that. It was the face. It was the hair. He was brave. When it was all said and done, I was absolutely convinced that Usher had delivered a gift," said L.A. Reid in the film.

DID YOU KNOW?
The first completely 3-D movie shown to an audience was in 1922—almost 100 years ago! The movie was called The Power of Love.

The film shows the indefatigable efforts of Bieber as he got the word out about his music. He traveled all across the country visiting local radio stations and performing live for small audiences. "There's not a DJ

Justin Bieber attends the UK Premiere of *Justin Bieber: Never Say Never* at Cineworld 02 Arena on February 16, 2011, in London, England.

Fans are seen at the premiere of Paramount Pictures' 'Justin Bieber: Never Say Never' held at Nokia Theater L.A. Live on February 8, 2011, in Los Angeles, California.

TEST YOUR JB IQ

1. Name the artist who did not appear as a special guest in Justin's August 31, 2010, concert, as featured in *Justin Bieber: Never Say Never*.
- *Usher, Jaden Smith, Ludacris, Akon, Miley Cyrus*

2. Aside from the WNBA's New York Liberty, Madison Square Garden is home to two sports teams. Name them.

3. In which film did the song "Never Say Never" first appear?

4. What hit film did director Jon Chu helm before taking on *Justin Bieber: Never Say Never*?

5. You've seen the movie. Did you spot all the celebrities? Which famous face did not appear in *Justin Bieber: Never Say Never*?
- *Lionel Richie, Adrian Grenier, Adam Levine, David Beckham, Will Smith*

Answers: 1-Akon, 2-New York Knicks and New York Rangers, 3-The Karate Kid (2010), 4-Step Up 3D, 5-Adam Levine

that could say they have not met Justin Bieber," Scooter Braun says.

Bieber's rise to fame may have come quickly, but it wasn't without hard work. Ryan Good, Bieber's road manager and man-at-arms, reflects, "It went naturally, but naturally doesn't mean easy. There's work that goes into that—and you have to do the footwork."

The footwork paid off—in spades. Randy Phillips, AEG tour promoter finds Bieber's

THIS DAY IN JB-ISTORY
Justin Bieber: Never Say Never *premeries in more than 3,000 theaters across America, taking in almost $30 million on opening weekend alone!*

FEBRUARY 11, 2011

feat staggering. "All these giant artists who sell out arenas every two or three years when they go on tour...Justin's one of them now. On his first record. In his first year and a half. I don't believe that's ever happened," he said.

The movie also opens a window into a very peculiar world: life for a teenager on the road as a touring artist. "It becomes a very functional dysfunctional family, all centered around one goal," "Mama" Jan Smith

Chapter 10:
JUSTIN: THE MOVIE

reflects. Recognizing the difficulties of an inarguably abnormal existence, Justin's team feels a personal obligation to keep the singer grounded.

The movie culminates with Bieber's performance in front of a sold-out crowd at Madison Square Garden in New York City. Performing at MSG is described as the pinnacle for a performing artist's career. Promoters were initially worried that Bieber might not get a sellout at the huge venue. He did—selling to capacity within only 22 minutes of tickets going on sale.

All of the flash-whiz-bang of Justin's stage show comes through in living color. The slick choreography, the pyrotechnics, and the larger-than-life acrobatics of his dance crew—not to mention the palpable excitement of audiences—are all the more impressive in 3-D.

One of the most touching interludes in the film profiles two the Bieber camp's standard practices: offering free tickets to fans without tickets, and upgrading random families to front-row seats. Says Braun, "Me and the guy from *Extreme Makeover* have the best jobs in the world because we get to go out and make people happy."

"Justin's fans are the most loyal group of girls on the planet. They all feel a certain sense of ownership over him because they feel like they found him before Scooter found him, before the record labels found him. He belongs to *them*," said general manager Allison Kaye.

Justin Bieber: Never Say Never not only paints a portrait of Justin as a young artist and a person, but it also puts

JUSTIN'S FAVORITE THINGS!

SKATEBOARDS
LIFE ON TOUR CAN BE HECTIC, BUT GETTING FROM POINT A TO POINT B IS IMMINENTLY MORE FUN ON A SKATEBOARD, WHICH JUSTIN USES AS A FREQUENT MODE OF TRANSPORT.

Usher and Justin Bieber backstage before Justin Bieber performs at Madison Square Garden on August 31, 2010, in New York City.

a face to some of the countless fans who show up to concerts, buy his albums, and devote their time and attention to their favorite artist. The filmmakers give a voice to many of them, getting right to the heart of the phenomenon known as Bieber Fever and capturing the incomparable connection between the musician and his fans.

He's more than just a performer on stage; he has direct communication with his Beliebers. When the singer goes down with what might be a tour-threatening voice loss,

> ## UNDER THE INFLUENCE
>
> *Justin's idol, Michael Jackson, was the subject of his own documentary, released in 2009 and titled Michael Jackson's* This Is It. *The film went behind the scenes of Jackson's comeback tour. Sadly, the singer died before the tour could be completed.*

get-well wishes pour in from fans across the globe. More important, Justin hits them right back, expressing his regret at having to postpone a concert date and also thanking them for their support, encouragement, and understanding.

What emerges from the movie is a picture of an artist who works tirelessly for his craft, a true musician and entertainer whose commitment to his fan base is unparalleled. He's a kid with dreams that really did come true, and the inspiration to his followers is unquestionable.

BEHIND THE MUSIC

The music documentary has been around almost as long as documentaries themselves. Many great directors have gotten their starts filming concert documentaries, from Oscar winner Martin Scorsese, whose *The Last Waltz* was an early film, to Jonathan Demme (himself an Oscar winner), who has directed several of them in his illustrious career.

Recent documentary fare has taken advantage of a popular medium: 3-D.

Miley Cyrus hit theaters in 2007 with *Hannah Montana and Miley Cyrus: The Best of Both Worlds Concert.* The Jonas Brothers followed with an offering of their own in 2009: *Jonas Brothers: The 3D Concert Experience.* Both films were successful, but *Justin Bieber: Never Say Never* is the undisputed winner, raking in more than $100 million worldwide—compared to the JoBros' $30 million.

Justin Bieber attends the *Justin Bieber: Never Say Never* New York premiere at Regal E-Walk 13 on February 2, 2011, in New York City.

Justin Bieber performs at
Madison Square Garden on
August 31, 2010, in New York City.

THE CRITICS SPEAK

"It captures a genuine youthquake.... His grassroots rise is fascinating.... Playing the drums (he's a wizard), parading his kung fu fighting moves, he's the same boisterous, do-what-you-feel kid on stage that he was in those videos. That's why he leaves the Mileys and Jonases in the dust."—Owen Glieberman, *Entertainment Weekly*

"Chu's film reveals through home movies from Bieber's small Canadian town of Stratford, Ontario, early YouTube clips and interviews with the people who discovered him [that Bieber is] preternaturally gifted, freakishly poised, and incessantly hardworking. From the sense of rhythm he displayed at age two to his confident busking outside a theater at age 12 to the chutzpah he showed in approaching his eventual mentor, Usher, and offering to sing for him just a couple years ago, Bieber has always seemed fearless, yet somehow grounded. He couldn't be more contemporary, having built a grass-roots support system through social networks, and yet he has that old-fashioned thing called moxie. And he genuinely seems like a good kid—it's hard not to like him"—Christy Lemire, Associated Press

"An undeniably engaging musical portrait that delivers major bangs for the buck."—Michael Rechtshaffen, *Hollywood Reporter*

"*Justin Bieber: Never Say Never* makes a persuasive case for its titular star as a far more talented-than-usual teen idol."—Andrew Barker, *Variety*

"The movie is cunningly woven to show the tension between his insane success and his determination to remain a sane, normal 16-year-old.... Unlike most packaged teen idols, Bieber has a voice that needs no help from sound mixers, and home movies show he had uncannily slick moves from an early age."—David Edelstein, NPR

"A sweetly entertaining, canny celebration of the pop heartthrob du jour."—Jon Bream, *Minneapolis Star-Triubune*

Chapter 11:

AROUND THE WORLD

Chapter 11:
AROUND THE WORLD

The lights dim, the spotlights begin circle, and the place...explodes. Suddenly, thousands of fans are on their feet and screaming. They all came here for the same reason: Justin Bieber.

Seeing the star himself is enough to satisfy even the most rabid of fans. But the show itself is an impressive undertaking—filled with incredible set pieces, extremely complicated choreography, and plenty of fan interaction. "I want to show that I love to perform. There are going to be some cool tricks, some electronic things that haven't been seen before, for sure," he told the *Houston Chronicle* in an interview preceding a concert.

The stage show begins with the words everyone has on their mind, as the sample from the Cardigans' 1996 hit "Lovefool" begins: *Love me, love me...* Justin sings and dances his way across a huge stage complete with two levels of platforms, ramps, and catwalks. It's a high-energy show with lots of unique features. This is no Stratford Star, no YouTube living-room performance; everything is big, overblown.

At one point, Justin sails high across the audience in a giant metal rig in the shape of a heart. Suspended high in the air, he belts out the song "Never Let You Go," accompanying himself on acoustic guitar. As if that's not amazing enough, the rig is actually spinning through the air! In another memorable performance moment, he cruises tantalizingly close over the heads of his audience in a giant cage as he performs the song "Up."

But perhaps the most exciting moment—and the one that has become a signature of Justin's concerts—comes with the song "One Less Lonely Girl." For the performance, Justin chooses a single audience member from each concert and brings her on stage for a serenade. It's a romantic moment—and nearly every fan in the place waits with breathless anticipation to find out if she will be the one singled out.

There are so many different elements that add up to make this concert pure

127 CITIES

The number of cities in which Justin has performed on the My World tour since it began in June 2010.

> ## DID YOU KNOW?
>
> *You probably already know that Justin's touring act is huge, but did you know it takes eight buses and an entire fleet of 18-wheelers to move the singers, dancers, instruments, sound equipment, and sets from place to place?*

Singer Justin Bieber performs during his World Tour show at Madison Square Garden on August 31, 2010, in New York City.

Justin Bieber performs at Madison Square Garden on August 31, 2010, in New York City.

MATCH-MAKING

Match the artist with the leg of the My World tour on which they performed as opening act.

A. Jessica Jarrell
B. Willow Smith
C. Jasmine Villegas
D. Sean Kingston

Answers: A-3, B-1, C-2, D-4

spectacle. And as many of Justin's songs intimate, it's really a celebration of making one's dreams come true.

As the film *Justin Bieber: Never Say Never* quite accurately depicts, touring is a grueling business. In less than a year and a half, Justin will have traveled and performed in more than 100 cities in five continents. It's a tour schedule that not only puts a strain on a person's energy, but poses serious risks to damaging one's voice through exertion.

Justin found that out the hard way, when his tour hit the brakes in Syracuse in August 2010. Dog tired from performing in 37 cities in just over two months, and with a sore throat that seriously threatened laryngitis, the singer was forced to accept the inevitability of wear and tear on even the healthiest of bodies.

Luckily, he was able to quickly recover. After canceling the date, he was able to appear just two days later. "I'm tough. I'm Canadian," he tweeted. Justin credits those around him with keeping in performance condition. Describing Scooter and Usher in his autobiography, he wrote, "They're like tag team wrestlers, only instead of bashing me over the head with folding chairs they make me drink lots of water."

TWITTER-PATED:

That is how u end a tour!! Felt incredible. So grateful and still can't believe it. #myworldtour December 23, 2010.

Of course, they'd go on to extend the tour worldwide after that!

DECEMBER 23, 2010

Chapter 11:
AROUND THE WORLD

Justin gives credit where credit is due, pointing to his mentors who keep him focused and ready each day. One word of advice that Usher gave Justin near the beginning is something Justin can take to heart. Usher said, "Being the entertainer I am, I stand on the shoulders of giants that basically were trailblazers." It's something Justin knows all too well, and he has a massive respect for those "trailblazers" who came before him.

Hero Michael Jackson gets a tribute from Justin at all of his shows. When Justin takes time out to introduce his dancers and musicians one by one, they are accompanied by the sounds of Jackson's "Wanna Be Startin' Something." Justin calls

it "a celebration of Michael Jackson and a good reminder for me about what matters in this business."

Jackson has undoubtedly left a huge impression on Justin as a singer and performer, but there is another legacy that is just as influential: his commitment to philanthropy. "Michael Jackson was the most giving artist of all time," Justin writes in *First Step 2 Forever*. Inspired by Jackson's example, Justin wanted to make his own statement. For each ticket sold on the My World 2.0 tour, one dollar has been donated to Pencils of Promise.

As Pencils of Promise founder Adam Braun said in an interview with the *Hollywood Reporter*, every little bit adds up. "[Scooter] and Justin were able to turn several hundred thousand fans into several hundred thousand philanthropists with each of them giving one dollar to the organization." Through their direct efforts, they were able to build more than 15 schools with the proceeds gained from concert receipts.

With the world tour now wrapped for

Justin Bieber performs at Madison Square Garden on August 31, 2010, in New York City.

the moment, Justin is headed back into the studio to start recording his next effort. But there's little doubt that fans will be seeing him again very soon. "I have a great time performing," he told Philadelphia radio station Q102. Touring, after all, is the best way to connect with his millions of fans around the world. "At the end of the day, my fans are my everything, and they got me to this position," he once told MTV News.

"I think I can grow as an artist, and my fans will grow with me," he wrote in his official bio. Justin shows no signs of stopping, and neither does Bieber Fever. His millions of satisfied concertgoers would echo his words from *First Step 2 Forever:* "This is just the beginning.

JUSTIN STOOD HERE!

During a break in his world tour, Justin made a trek to one of the oldest sites in the world: Israel. He tweeted his excitement about being in such a special place: "Just amazing place...not a bad day. just wish got a little more space and privacy from the paps to enjoy this time with my family. Thanks," he wrote. "I'm in the holy land and i am grateful for that. I just want to have the same personal experience that others have here."

Justin's tour of the holy land, unfortunately, wasn't to be. After being hounded by photographers rabid to get a picture of the singer touring the sites, he was unable to complete his pilgrimage. "Staying in the hotel for the rest of the week u happy?" he tweeted the following day. "People wait their whole lives for opportunities like this, why would they want to take that experience away from someone. They should be ashamed of themselves. Take pictures of me eating but not in a place of prayer, ridiculous."

He was particularly upset that the photographers didn't show any reverence in religious sites. "You would think paparazzi would have some respect in holy places," he lamented. "All I wanted was the chance to walk where Jesus did here in Israel."

It was an unfortunate way to spoil what could have been a significant journey. But props to the Biebs for putting the paps in their place!

Justin's got Earth covered in tour dates. Next stop, the moon?

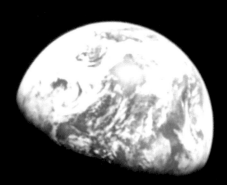

WHERE DID YOU SEE JUSTIN?

The My World tour keeps going...and going. Check out the tour stops Justin has hit so far.

Hartford, CT
Trenton, NJ
Cincinnati, OH
Milwaukee, WI
Minneapolis, MN
Des Moines, IA
Moline, IA
Omaha, NE
Grand Prairie, TX
Tulsa, OK
Broomfield, CO
W. Valley City, UT
Everett, WA
Portland, OR
Oakland, CA
Reno, NV
Los Angeles, CA
Paso Robles, CA
Las Vegas, NV
Glendale, AZ
Kansas City, MO
N. Little Rock, AK
Memphis, TN
Lafayette, LA
Orlando, FL
Sunrise, FL
Charlotte, NC
Duluth, GA
Nashville, TN
Indianapolis, IN
Columbus, OH
Auburn Hills, MI
Toronto, ON
London, ON
Ottawa, ON

Albany, NY
Providence, RI
Newark, NJ
Syracuse, NY
New York, NY
Manchester, NH
Essex Junction, VT
Allentown, PA
Timonium, MD
Winnipeg, MB
Regina, SK
Saskatoon, SK
Edmonton, AB
Calgary, AB
Vancouver, BC
Sacramento, CA
Ontario, CA
Los Angeles, CA
Anaheim, CA
San Jose, CA
San Diego, CA
Oklahoma City, OK
San Antonio, TX
Houston, TX
St. Louis, MO
Louisville, KY
Cleveland, OH
Norfolk, VA
Philadelphia, PA
Boston, MA TD
East Rutherford, NJ
Atlantic City, NJ
Montreal, QC
Toronto, ON
Pittsburgh, PA
Greensboro, NC
Greenville, SC
Miami, FL
Tampa, FL
Birmingham, AL

Atlanta, GA
Birmingham, England
Dublin, Ireland
Liverpool, England
Newcastle, England
London, England
Manchester, England
Sheffield, England
Nottingham, England
Oberhausen, Germany
Rotterdam, Holland
Paris, France
Antwerp, Belgium
Herning, Denmark
Berlin, Germany
Madrid, Spain
Barcelona, Span
Zurich, Switzerland
Milan, Italy
Tel Aviv, Israel
Singapore
Kuala Lumpur, Malaysia
Bogor, Indonesia
Brisbane, Australia
Sydney, Australia
Melbourne, Australia
Adelaide, Australia
Perth, Australia
Manila, Philippines
Chep Lap Kok, Hong Kong
Taipei, Taiwan
Osaka, Japan
Tokyo, Japan
Monterrey, Mexico
Mexico City, Mexico
Rio de Janiero, Brazil
Porto Alegre, Brazil
Buenos Aires, Argentina
Santiago, Chile
Lima, Peru

Chapter 12:

"THE GREATEST FANS IN THE WORLD"

Chapter 12:
"THE GREATEST FANS IN THE WORLD"

There's no argument: fan support can either make or break an artist. And as Justin has shown every step of the way in his career, his fans have paved the way for him. It was the fans, showing up in increased numbers on YouTube to comment and request more videos, who got Justin noticed by entertainment executives. It was the fans who made Justin into a multiplatinum-selling recording artist and the most powerful Twitter celebrity in the world.

The musician, who has repeatedly credited his fans with his success, sees it this way: "I don't think of myself as powerful. If anything, my fans are powerful. It's all in their hands. If they don't buy my albums, I go away," he told *Rolling Stone*.

It's not just that Justin's fans are buying his albums. They're doing so much more. Just as Justin is *the* trailblazing musician of the Internet age, his fans have taken their support and interaction to different levels than have ever been reached before. It all starts with Twitter.

$40,668

When the haircut heard around the world happened, Justin put his famed locks to good use, selling them on eBay and donating the proceeds to charity. Fans made a big statement, and the hair went for a pretty penny!

Justin, an early adopter of the social-networking site, has shown just how much can be accomplished through tweeting. He has stretched the boundaries of the medium—using it as a tour diary and window into his personality but also utilizing it as a publicity platform. His 12 million Twitter followers will be the first to hear all of his announcements—from updates on new songs and albums to tour news to charitable efforts. Through Twitter (and other Web sites, such as his official JustinBieberMusic.com), the fans are always the first ones to know.

Perhaps it is the personal aspect of Twitter—and the interaction that Justin has with his fans via the medium—that really empowers his fan base. And they have shown just how powerful they can be as a result.

Take Justin's 17th birthday as an example. Announcing his affiliation with the nonprofit organization Charity:Water, Justin wrote on the charity's Web site, "This year, I really want my birthday to be all about helping

> ## QUOTABLE *JUSTIN*
>
> *"Every fan is so special to me. I love being in the studio, but not as much as I love performing live because that's when I get to connect with [my fans]."*
>
> **—Justin, writing in First Step 2 Forever about the significance of his fans**

A Philippine fan of Canadian teen idol Justin Bieber shouts during the one-night concert in Manila on May 10, 2011, as part of Bieber's world tour.

Justin Bieber performs at his 'My World Tour' at Nokia Live on July 20, 2010, in Los Angeles, California.

SPOTLIGHT ON CAROLINE GONZALEZ

If you could be mayor of your hometown for one day, what would you do? That's the question that Caroline Gonzalez, age 11, got to answer when she won a Facebook contest in her hometown of Forney, Texas. The contest, designed to promote young people's interest in local government, was sponsored by the town, which named her mayor for the day.

Her first order of business? Renaming the town's main street after her musical inspiration: Justin Bieber. When asked what her reasoning was behind the big mayoral decision, Gonzalez said, "I like his music and I like him. And I thought, *Why not have a street in my hometown named after my favorite singer?*""

So if you find yourself in Forney, Texas, anytime soon, you'll be able to cruise down Justin Bieber Way yourself.

others. Instead of asking for gifts, I'm asking friends, family, and fans to consider donating $17 for my 17th birthday to help make a change. One hundred percent of all donations go directly to building clean water projects in developing countries."

And then he took the announcement to Twitter. The response was enormous. As Charity:Water tweeted, "Thanks to all you Beliebers, we hit $7 million raised on mycharity: water today! #makeachange."

TWITTER-PATED:

"something else i saw i liked in a book a fan gave me was B.I.E.B.E.R. = Believe In Everything Because Everything Is Reachable. love that."

JANUARY 3, 2011

The Twitter tag #makeachange has been particularly special to Justin. Perhaps a nod to Michael Jackson and his influential song "Man in the Mirror" (which includes the lyric "gonna make a change"), Bieber has used the hashtag as a call to arms for his fans. Justin's grassroots campaign for charitable causes has caused a ripple effect among the Bieber faithful. They have followed his example and taken that philosophy of making a change to heart.

Chapter 12:
"THE GREATEST FANS IN THE WORLD"

Often, their charitable efforts get the attention of the performer.

One group of Beliebers in Buffalo, New York, helped #makeachange in their own town. Raising funds for its local children's hospital, the fans collected more than $200,000 in charitable donations from their community—all of it in pennies. "the fans in Buffalo raised $200k in pennies for charity...that is 20 Million Pennies!!! WOW!! VERY PROUD!!" Bieber tweeted about the feat.

Fans have also used their social-networking connections to organize efforts on the singer's behalf. In September 2011 a prankster made false copyright claims to YouTube, alleging that the official Justin Bieber channel (along with official channels for fellow artists Lady Gaga and Rihanna, among others) was broadcasting

VOCABULARY

hashtag ('hash · tag)
Popularized on Twitter, the hashtag is designed to group tweets by a common theme. Thus, Twitter followers searching a specific topic can find related tweets easily by searching a specific hashtag.

unauthorized content. YouTube's official policy is to pull any content in dispute, and the channel disappeared. Almost immediately, a posse of Bieber fans were on the case, and helped to bring the false claim to YouTube's attention and resolve the issue quickly.

The Bieber faithful have an Internet presence all their own. Fans from all over the world have paid tribute to their beloved, creating Web sites devoted to the musician and his music: posting YouTube tribute videos, fan fiction, and poetry; and creating online communities where fans can congregate and communicate with one another.

They've also shown their numbers physically, gathering wherever the star goes.

Beliebers in Newcastle, England, celebrating the star's arrival before his upcoming concert, began an impromptu parade down the city's streets, singing Bieber's music and

JUSTIN'S FAVORITE THINGS!

A FAMILIAR SIGHT AT JUSTIN BIEBER CONCERTS, THE SINGER LOVES SEEING HIS FANS HOLDING THEIR HANDS IN THE SHAPE OF A HEART.

Fans screamed at the TD Garden as the start of Justin Bieber's concert approached.

Chapter 12:
"THE GREATEST FANS IN THE WORLD"

promenading through the city with signs and banners heralding his arrival.

Fans in Sydney took it even further. The massive crowd of enthusiastic fans awaiting a morning performance at Circular Quay at Sydney Harbor swelled so large outside the gates that it turned into a stampede. Police were forced to postpone the performance. "I am just as disappointed as everyone else with the news from this morning. I want to sing for my fans," Bieber tweeted. "I woke up this morning to the police canceling the show for safety reasons.... I love my fans... I love it here in Australia...and I want to sing." A similar near-riot broke out months earlier at Roosevelt Field Mall in Long Island, New York.

The singer, reflecting on the phenomenon of Bieber Fever to MTV News, said, "I think it's my fans being really supportive. They made [the phrase] up. At the end of the day, my fans are my everything, and they got me to this position." From the looks of it, Bieber Fever shows no signs of stopping anytime soon.

THIS DAY IN JB-ISTORY

Based on the enthusiastic reception from fans for his My World 2.0 album, Justin receives his first-ever platinum album certification from the Recording Industry Association of America.

NOVEMBER 17, 2010

I'M A BELIEBER

Fans of Justin Bieber are everywhere. They come from every walk of life and from countries around the world. So it's little wonder that this special group of fans is known by a multitude of different names.

The most often-heard moniker for fans of the Biebs is **Beliebers**, and the fans are fervent in their faith that the musician can do it all.

The **Bieber Army** stands millions strong. The **Bieberites** are acolytes of the singer and his music.

And the **Bieberphiles**, no surprise, live up to their moniker; they really do love Justin Bieber.

From **Bieber Babes** to **Bieb Boys**, whatever the name, the fans have demonstrated that they are a powerful force indeed.

Singer Justin Bieber makes a heart sign to fans outside of the Nintendo World Store on September 1, 2009, in New York City.

Fans of singer Justin Bieber kiss his wax figure during a ceremony to unveil the figure of the teen sensation at Madame Tussauds in New York, March 15, 2011.

JB LIBS

You and _____ are so _____. You're going to a Justin Bieber
       [friend's name]   [adjective]

concert in _____ .
        [place]

To get ready, you gather your _____ and _____. As you
        [plural noun]   [noun]

_____ rush out the door, you hear a _____.
[adverb]   [sound]

"What's that _____?" asks your friend.
        [sound]

You pause and _____. You hear the sound again and feel _____.
        [verb]   [mood]

Leaving the house, you see something strange. You _____ and it's...
        [verb]

Justin Bieber.

"Hi," he says _____.
      [adverb]

You _____. "_____! Justin Bieber! Is it really you?"
     [verb]   [Exclamation]

"I need some help from my fans with _____," he says.
            [noun]

_____ hours later, you are on stage with Justin, [active verb].
[Number]

"Let me introduce my _____ friends to you," he says.
         [adjective]

You [verb], and the crowd erupts in a/an _____ cheer.
            [adjective]

It is the _____ moment of your life.
    [adjective]

Chapter 13:

JUSTIN BIEBER: FASHION PLATE

Chapter 13:
JUSTIN BIEBER: FASHION PLATE

Lady Gaga might get credit for being music's reigning fashionista, but her contemporary Justin Bieber has a signature style all his own. You probably won't ever see Justin wearing raw meat, but he definitely pushes the boundaries of what fashion means for a pop musician.

Speaking of Mama Monster's sartorial choices at the 2010 VMAs, Bieber told Chelsea Handler, "She went for a hug, and I was like, 'Ooohhh, let's just hold up on that, you have meat on you." When Handler asked him if he liked the meat dress or the egg costume better, Bieber replied, "I thought both were weird. People say it's artistic and stuff. I'm just like, 'You're an egg.'"

Leave it to Justin to point out the fine line between being edgy and being... weird. Unlike the pop idols of his youth—like Boyz II Men, with their carefully choreographed and well-scrubbed styles—there's something of an edge to the clothes Justin wears on stage. It all starts with Ryan Good, Justin's so-called "swagger coach" and stylist.

For the My World tours, his on-stage ensemble has a heavy element of street style, and highlights the singer's signature color: purple. For his main look, Bieber wears a white denim jacket embellished with straps and metal hardware. The look is heavily influenced by hip-hop elements. Paired with white jeans speckled with purple, the look is crisp but definitely not clean-cut. A studded belt picks up the stud accents on his jacket and ties together the look. Add a splash of purple from the hoodie layered underneath, plus the purple Supra Skytop sneakers and a purple baseball cap (his dancers wear the same purple cap, too) and the look is complete. It's a look that's

> ### QUOTABLE *JUSTIN*
>
> *"Style can be how you carry yourself and how you wear whatever you have on. I like to consider my style as very relatable."*
>
> —Justin writing in First Step 2 Forever

JUSTIN'S *FAVORITE THINGS!*

HE HAS MORE SNEAKERS THAN HE CAN COUNT, BUT HE HAS OFTEN SAID THAT HIS FAVORITES ARE SUPRA SKYTOPS.

Justin Bieber and Selena Gomez arrive at the The 28th Annual MTV Video Music Awards at Nokia Theatre L.A. LIVE on August 28, 2011, in Los Angeles, California.

Justin Bieber, Pattie Mallette, and Editor-In-Chief of American *Vogue* Anna Wintour attend the Dolce & Gabbana celebration during Fashion's Night Out at Dolce & Gabbana Boutique on September 8, 2011, in New York City.

JUSTIN GETS ICED

Talk about some bling! Leave it to Justin to interpret the glitz of hip-hop style with his own flair. In May 2011 he stepped out wearing some very original jewelry: a jewel-encrusted pendant in the shape of *The Family Guy*'s Stewie. The pendant, set in 14-karat gold, contains over 12 karats of precious gems, including rubies and diamonds.

The singer reportedly designed the pendant in co-operation with Beverly Hills jeweler Jason Arashben.

According to estimates, the bling is estimated to be worth $25,000! As Stewie Griffin would say, *What the deuce!*

unmistakably Bieber.

Justin has become known for his preference for Supra sneakers, and a well-worn pair that he broke in on stage was recently enshrined in Toronto's Bata Shoe Museum. The museum, which features shoes worn by such musical notables as John Lennon and Madonna, hosts a collection of footwear from throughout the ages—everything from Napoleon Bonaparte's socks to Queen Victoria's slippers. Talk about putting your best foot forward!

Considering his look from head to toe (or more appropriately, from toe to head), Justin makes a statement with his headgear. Whether on stage or just hanging out, he's often sporting a hat. Most often, it's a baseball cap. Often, it's in support of the New York Yankees baseball team. Besides the Yankees' traditional blue, the singer has donned turquoise, black, and purple versions of the cap. But don't assume he's a die-hard fanatic of the Bronx Bombers; he's also worn ballcaps for his now-home-town Atlanta Braves, as well as the Detroit Tigers.

Another one of Justin's favorite fashion accessories is glasses. The singer has showcased a wide array of spectacles on the red carpet and on the street. He's rocked huge, chunky-framed eyeglasses and other

SAY WHAT?

"I want you to know you are all the way beautiful, even with those...lesbian bangs."

—Kathy Griffin, joking with the singer in a YouTube video

Chapter 13:
JUSTIN BIEBER: FASHION PLATE

spectacles in black and white. He has recently been seen sporting wire-rimmed specs, as featured at the 2011 VMAs. The singer reportedly has perfect vision; the glasses are purely a style choice.

He's also often seen in sunglasses, a true staple accessory for any celebrity. In fact, the 3-D glasses for his film, *Justin Bieber: Never Say Never* were modeled after a style he favors. The glasses, with chunky plastic frames in—what else?—purple, were given to moviegoers who saw the concert film in 3-D.

Most often, the singer showcases a laid-back style, wearing hoodies, T-shirts, and jeans—and turning up the volume with a selection from his ever-expanding collection of sneakers. If it seems like the singer has a pair in every color of the rainbow, it's probably because he does!

Lately, the singer's style has become more sophisticated. Perhaps it's because he's growing up and finding his own fashion identity. Or maybe it has something to do with his current girlfriend, Selena Gomez—herself an established fashionista and bona fide sophisticate. The two

first glammed it up as a couple when they stepped out for the first time together—to no dressier an occasion than the Oscar post-parties. In an interview before the 2011 MTV Video Music Awards, Selena interviewed Justin about his red-carpet fashion. The singer walked the white carpet wearing a dressed-up but very rock 'n' roll look, including a Yves St. Laurent tuxedo jacket, brooch, and cheetah-print sneakers paired with red pants. Perhaps Selena's taste for couture is rubbing off on him.

Of course, no assessment of Justin's style would be complete without a discussion of his most-talked-about style feature: his hairstyle. Justin's famous 'do has been the subject of countless ruminations. It was even adapted into a wig—a hot-selling costume accessory. Bieber's hairstylist, Vanessa Price, had a big hand in shaping

HAIR APPARENT

Justin's hair is one hot topic. Justin Bieber: Never Say Never even features a short montage of Justin's signature hair flips—and the coup de grace: the flip in slow-mo. "He has prettier hair than I do," says Miley Cyrus.

the performer's forward-swept style. And when he decided to change it, Price was there, scissors in hand.

"[T[hinking about getting a haircut....hmmmmmm," the singer tweeted to his fans on February 21, 2011. The singer, known for his practical joking, had fans on the ropes.

Actress Selena Gomez and musician Justin Bieber attend the 2011 Vanity Fair Oscar Party Hosted by Graydon Carter at the Sunset Tower Hotel on February 27, 2011, in West Hollywood, California.

Chapter 13:
JUSTIN BIEBER: FASHION PLATE

Was he serious? Two months earlier he told Barbara Walters, "I think after my movie I might cut my hair a little shorter." Then he reversed himself in January 2011, telling Matt Lauer, "I am not shaving it off" but instead was having fun "just messing it up a lot."

But cut it he did. The cut is "suitable for a young man instead of a teenage boy," Price told *Elle* magazine. Adding, "the world had never seen it before," speaking about his forehead.

When asked by Disney Radio if Bieber's power lay in his hair, Selena Gomez said, "I don't think it's the hair.... He's got game. He knows what he's doing."

And now it seems he's stepping up his game in more ways than one. There's little doubt his music will mature right along with him and his style.

> ## TWITTER-PATED:
>
> ### "yeah so it's true...i got a lil haircut...i like it."
>
> **FEBRUARY 21, 2011**

F-F-F-FASHION!

While Justin's fashion choices have influenced his Beliebers, many of his fans prefer to wear their hearts on their sleeves—literally. Justin Bieber apparel is a cottage industry all its own, and Bieber-branded clothing is available in retail stores everywhere.

Justin's own Web site, JustinBieber-Music.com, offers a variety of clothing options to fans. Want a purple hoodie like the one Justin wears on stage? They've got you covered. Need a pair of monogrammed lounge pants to get cozy in? Check. From headbands to hats to T-shirts, his homepage is a one-stop shop for the singer's swag.

Stop in any retail chain from Claire's Accessories to Sears and you're likely to see the musician's face emblazoned on a T-shirt. Little wonder, then, that each stop on the Biebs' tour features plenty of Bieber-bedecked fans.

There are even some celebrity Beliebers rocking his image, too. The actress Tiffani Thiessen wore a Justin Bieber T-shirt on the red carpet for the Los Angeles premiere of *Horrible Bosses*. Justin had recently worn a T-shirt featuring Thiessen in her role as Kelly Kapowski on the 1990s sitcom *Saved By the Bell*. "Thanks for the love, Justin Bieber," she tweeted.

Musician Justin Bieber attends
the 2011, CMT Music Awards at the
Bridgestone Arena on June 8, 2011,
in Nashville, Tennessee.

MADE IN THE SHADES

The eyes have it! Can you tell which photos are Bieber and which aren't?

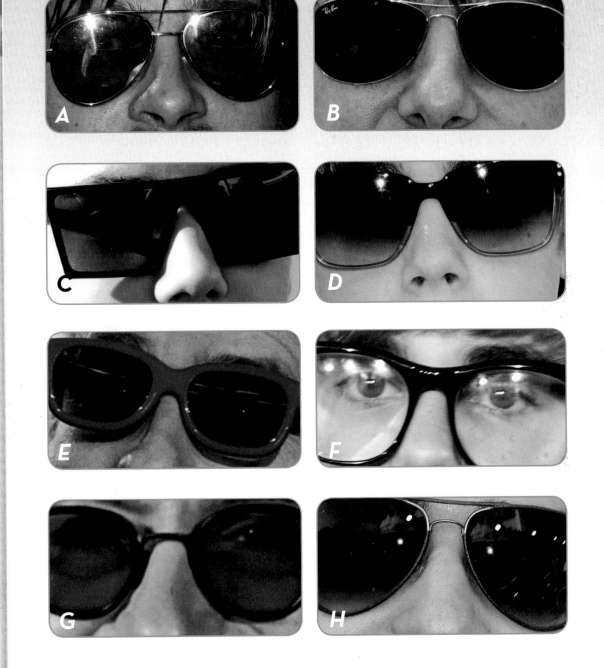

Answers: A-Brad Pitt; B-Tom Cruise; C-Justin Bieber; D-Justin Bieber; E-German talk-show host Thomas Gottschalk tried on the purple 3-D glasses; F-Justin Bieber G-Robert Downey Jr. H-Justin Timberlake

Chapter 14:
THE MERCH

Chapter 14:
THE MERCH

If it seems like everywhere you go these days you see Justin's name, you're probably not going crazy. Besides his wildly successful career as a musician—which has him in the press practically every day—he has also vastly expanded his branding empire. To put it simply, Bieber is a household name in every sense of the term.

Forget the fashion. Bieber's official Web site offers gadgets and gizmos for every Belieber in your life. Got a friend who's positively attached to her phone? You've got your choice of Bieber-themed iPhone skins. What about that person on your list who loves to travel? Why not pick up the Justin Bieber Travel Kit—or better yet, the singing toothbrush that croons "Somebody to Love" and "Love Me" as you brush your pearly whites. And don't forget the dental floss!

From hoodies to headbands, plushees to posters, T-shirts to toys, Bieber has lent his name to a variety of products. He even has his own iPhone app. And fans simply keep waiting for more!

Fans can literally cozy up to Justin as they sleep—with bed linens and comforters designed by Lady Sandra Home Bedding. And fans that find Justin to be a living doll can have a miniaturized version of the singer himself. The collectible likenesses feature mini-Justin wearing a variety of looks from his videos, including fashions from "Baby" and "One Less Lonely Girl."

For the Christmas season in 2010, he premiered a nail polish line for female fans. Working with cosmetic giant OPI, each nail polish shade bears a name inspired by one of Justin's songs. From "One Less Lonely Glitter" to "Prized Possession Purple" and "Step 2 the Beat of My Heart." The shades were an instant hit for Wal-Mart, the exclusive retailer, selling more than 1 million bottles in their first month and selling out nationwide. The line has since expanded from its initial six shades to 14 different colors, and is now available in stores across the nation.

$3 MILLION

Sales for Someday in its first three weeks! It's "the biggest celebrity fragrance launch on record," according to Macy's chairman Terry Lundgren.

QUOTABLE JUSTIN

"I'm more concerned about how girls smell 'cause I'm a guy and I know what smells good and I know what I like. So girls should know, if [I like] it, then other guys are going to like it."

—Bieber to MTV News at the Someday fragrance launch in New York

Justin Bieber attends the Justin Bieber fragrance launch at Macy's Herald Square on June 23, 2011, in New York City.

Kaci Nuyen 8, holds a Justin Bieber Singing Doll during a Hamleys Christmas toy photocall at Hamleys Toy Store on June 28, 2011, in London, England.

BEHIND THE MUSIC

Justin has never been shy about crediting the Internet with increasing his profile and launching his musical career. In a recent ad for Google Chrome, the singer pays homage to his Internet roots by lending his life story to the advertiser.

The commercial is like a mini-*Justin Bieber: Never Say Never*. It traces a computer user who logs on to YouTube as "kidrauhl" and posts a little video of Justin singing at a talent competition. The commercial goes on to show the YouTube comments stream in and the views climb. It goes on to trace the musician's rise to fame through the lens of the Internet—music videos, Twitter, tour stops, and concert footage. Taking a step back and seeing how it all developed in such a short time is staggering.

If anyone's life story could read as a personal testament to the power of the Internet in this increasingly digital age, it could be Justin. Fitting, then, that the commercial's tagline is "The web is what you make of it."

Paired with the nail polish, Justin put his own spin on the typical celebrity fragrance venture. Partnering with Etoile Nation Beauty, he launched a line of scented wristbands and dog tags bearing four unisex scents. The products use a recent innovative technology: a patented resin that will hold the scent for up to a year. The "My World" accessories each bear the singer's name and face, and come in fragrances with names inspired by the singer's personality. Sold at Wal-Mart stores, the products have been another huge seller.

Having conquered fragrances with his innovative accessories, he bowed his first traditional perfume in June 2011. As Justin described to *Today*, I'm more interested in how females smell than males, which is why I decided to do it for all the girls, and 100 percent of the proceeds go to charity."

The launch for Someday for women, held at Macy's

SAY WHAT?

"In a recession, the last thing people want to hear about is entitlement. They want to hear about hard work, a successful story, and 'the American Dream.' And funny enough that 'the American Dream' came from some kid in Canada."

Chapter 14:
THE MERCH

flagship store in New York City, attracted massive crowds of fans, many of whom had camped out all night—in the rain—for a glimpse of the singer, who was on hand to sign autographs and shill his latest product. The fragrance is described by the distributor, "energy with a state-of-mind that inspires. It is a personal gift straight from his heart, giving fans a chance to get one step closer to Justin. It's a fragrance he can't get enough of and can't stay away from, making those who wear it irresistible." Little wonder, then, that so many lined up to get their hands on it first.

He teamed with legendary rapper Dr. Dre recently to release his own brand of Beats, the Dre-developed headphones that have become increasingly popular in the digital music age.

TRUE / *NOT TRUE?*

Justin released an iPhone app to accompany his Someday fragrance launch.

True. As they say, "Yep, there's an app for that."

Justin's Beats are—surprise!—purple and chrome. Touted with the tagline "sound is the emotion between us," come in on-ear headphones and in-ear varieties.

And if that collaboration isn't surprising enough, he's also recently signed with the Middleton family (yes, as in Princess Kate!), who own an online party-planning business called Party Pieces. The Web site purchased rights to sell the "Justin Bieber Ultimate Party Kit," a veritable Bieber party in a box.

He's inked endorsement deals with a number of retailers, including Xbox and remains an ardent fan of the *video game* system's offerings, most recently NBA 2K, Call of Duty: Black Ops, Marvel vs. DC, and Madden 2011. (His head of security Kenny Hamilton is "a frequent victim of [his] Xbox 360 powers of

JUSTIN'S FAVORITE THINGS!

JUSTIN SEEMS TO BE ALL EARS FOR HIS NEW JUSTBEATS. THE SINGER HAS BEEN SPOTTED ALL OVER WEARING HIS PERSONALIZED HEADPHONES.

Tiffani Thiessen attends the screening of *Horrible Bosses* at Sunshine Landmark on June 23, 2011, in New York City.

annihilation," as Justin wrote in his memoir.) He also joined fellow recording stars Katy Perry and Jessica Simpson, among others, as a recent face of Proactiv, the skincare and acne-prevention product line.

For the ad blitz of Super Bowl XLV—with commercials going for a pretty penny at $3 million for a 30-second spot—Best Buy ran an ad with Justin and famous rocker Ozzy Osbourne. The commercial, a play on the technology gap between generations, ended up being one of the most memorable—and hilarious—of the day.

One might think that with all these

> ### DID YOU KNOW?
>
> *Justin isn't the first celebrity to work with OPI. Fellow recording artist Katy Perry and tennis superstar Serena Williams have also developed shades for the nail polish brand.*

products and advertisements out on the market, Justin has reached his media-saturation point, but his Q score—the standard numeric index of a celebrity's popularity, as used by advertisers—remains on solid footing.

Rumors keep swirling about Justin's next ventures. He's reportedly had talks to open his own retail store. He's also hinted that he'd like a shoe line someday.

With all of these irons in the fire, it's easy to see why Justin has become one of the top celebrity earners. But with so much of it going to charity, Justin is far from cashing in. He's putting a new meaning to "pay it

JUSTIN REACHES OUT

Forbes may count Justin among its highest earners in celebrity endorsements, but for all he earns, he gives back a substantial amount. It's one of the many things that got him noticed by the philanthropic group Do Something. But for Justin it's more than that. It's a personal commitment to give back.

On New Year's Eve in 2010, Justin tweeted, "so my #newyearsresolution is to continue to give back for my blessings and do more than the year

before. i wanna #makeachange." And so far, Justin has put his money where his mouth is. One hundred percent of proceeds from Someday will be donated to various charities from Justin's favorite, Pencils of Promise, to the Make-A-Wish Foundation.

There's no doubt that Justin has demonstrated a strong willingness to help people in need. "I can make a difference in this world," he writes in *First Step 2 Forever*. "That's what this is all about."

Atmosphere for Justin Bieber as he performs part of his My World tour 2010 at the Reno Events Center on July 18, 2010, in Reno, Nevada.

Canadian singer Justin Bieber and his mother Pattie Mallette arrive at Taoyuan International Airport on May 15, 2011, in Taoyuan, Taiwan, Republic of China.

TEST YOUR JB IQ

1. Which one of these shades is not in OPI's Bieber line?

    A: OMB!

    B: One Time Lime

    C: Step 2 the Beat of My Heart

    D: Love 2 See U Smile

2. What product is not part of the Justin Bieber Ultimate Party Kit sold by Party Pieces?

    A. Plates

    B. Napkins

    C. Utensils

    D. Balloons

3. For how much does a 3.4 ounce bottle of Someday fragrance retail?

    A. $25

    B. $35

    C. $45

    D. $55

4. Which celebrity has not done product endorsements for Proactiv?

    A. Jordin Sparks

    B. Alicia Keys

    C. P. Diddy

    D. Avril Lavigne

5. Fans can buy a Bieber doll sporting the look from which music video?

    A. "U Smile"

    B. "One Time"

    C. "Never Say Never"

    D. "Favorite Girl"

6. What is the name of the headphones created by Justin and Dr. Dre's Beats?

    A. JustBeats

    B. BieberBeats

    C. Justin's Beats

    D. JBeats

7. Which one of these is not a scent in Justin's My World collection of fragrance-infused dog tags and wristbands?

    A. Icon

    B. Energy

    C. Superstar

    D. Tour

Answers: 1-D; 2-C; 3-D; 4-A; 5-B; 6-A; 7-C

Chapter 15:

JUSTIN GIVES BACK

Chapter 15:
JUSTIN GIVES BACK

Fame is a tricky thing. With a vast team of managers, producers, crew, and other entourage members surrounding a singer, it's tempting for artists to believe that the world revolves around them. Justin Bieber is *not* one of those art-

ists. He has shown time and again that he is committed to giving back. And he gives and gives—not only through financial contributions but with his time. For a kid whose own grueling touring schedule and other commitments already wear him thin, his insistence on making charity a top priority is commendable.

His tireless philanthropic efforts earned him a 2010 Do Something Award and a 2010 Power of Youth Philanthropy Award from *Variety*—impressive accolades for the then–16-year-old. The awards recognized not only the singer's personal contributions, but also the influence he had on others to get involved. Indeed, Justin's charitable spirit has caused a ripple

effect throughout his fan base, galvanizing a whole generation of Beliebers to think globally about giving.

Justin has used his musical talent to contribute to a number of charitable causes in his short career. In January 2010 a devastating earthquake hit the island of Haiti, causing widespread destruction and claiming more than 300,000 lives. Artists across the United States answered the call, recording a new version of "We Are the World" to help raise funds to aid rebuilding efforts. The original song, written by Lionel Richie and Michael Jackson and conceived as a charitable effort to send aid to a poverty-stricken Africa, became the top-selling single of all time. In the 25th anniversary version, Justin was given the honor of the song's opening solo. Benefiting the Red Cross, the new single brought much-needed funds to tragedy-stricken Haitians.

Participating was a no-brainer for Justin, who felt the call to action. The fringe

VOCABULARY
altruism ('al·trü·,i·zəm)
An unselfish regard or devotion to the needs of others

benefit was standing alongside some true giants of the recording industry. "[It] was incredible.... I got to work with...all the greats.... Barbra Streisand was on one side

Justin Bieber (L) and Scooter Braun attend Variety's 4th annual Power of Youth event at Paramount Studios on October 24, 2010, in Hollywood, California.

Justin Bieber accepts the Do Something Music Artist award onstage during the 2011 VH1 Do Something Awards at the Hollywood Palladium on August 14, 2011, in Hollywood, California.

SPOTLIGHT ON PENCILS OF PROMISE

If there is one organization with which Justin is mostly closely associated, it is no doubt Pencils of Promise. The nonprofit, started by Scooter Braun's brother Adam Braun, is a labor of love. While backpacking through 50 countries across the world as a 27-year-old, Adam saw the need for change firsthand. "In India, I asked a boy begging, 'If you could have anything, what would you want?' He said a pencil, so I gave him mine, and he exploded with this big smile and an overwhelming sense of possibility," Braun recounts. "It was an incredibly transformative moment for me," he told the *Hollywood Reporter*.

Returning to America, Braun quit his job in finance and started Pencils of Promise in 2009. The mission: to build schools and bring educational resources to the places that need it most. "That first pencil led to many pencils. Now, in every country I go to, I pass out pencils which lead to conversations, usually with parents.... Probably 80 to 90 percent of them are most concerned with education for their children. So that's always been my ambition." Braun continued.

When Justin joined the cause—most notably donating $1 from each concert ticket sold on his tour—things really took off. In April 2011, Braun and Bieber launched Schools 4 All, an effort to bring education to those among the 75 million children across the world without access to education. To date, Pencils of Promise has built more than 30 schools in Southeast Asia and Central America, with many more under way.

"I'm really blessed to be in this position," Bieber said at *Variety*'s Power of Youth event. "We really like the idea of youth helping out other youth."

of me and Celine Dion was on the other side of me and I felt like, *This is so big*."

When Mother Nature struck again—this time, in the form of an earthquake and tsunami that decimated wide swaths of Japan—Justin again felt the call. Teaming with artists Elton John, Beyonce, U2, Bob Dylan, and Eminem, among many others, Bieber lent a version of his song "Pray" to the album *Songs for Japan*. The proceeds went straight to the Japanese Red Cross and its rebuilding efforts.

Tweeting in 2010, Justin wrote, "I am

ART IMITATING LIFE

"'Pray' is one of my favorite songs I've ever recorded. It's very motivational and really inspiring. It definitely is able to touch people," Justin told Radio Disney. The song is very much a reflection of how Justin sees the world.

in the position to give back thanks to my fans and God. I wrote the track 'Pray' thinking I wanted to help others and I feel like I have a responsibility to do so. What is the point of doing all this if you can't make a difference in others' lives? This album is a gift to my fans and the money raised from it allows us all to help out."

"Pray," first recorded for the *My Worlds Acoustic* album, was borne from the singer's wish to give back—a desire he attributes in part to Michael Jackson, whose own "Man in the Mirror" inspired the song. Perhaps as a tribute to the King of Pop, Justin elected to donate a portion of the proceeds from sales of the album to the Children's Miracle Network, an organization that raises money for children's hospitals around the country. The musician is also recording a 2011 Christmas album. In what should come as no surprise, the proceeds from that effort will

UNDER THE INFLUENCE

Michael Jackson isn't the only role model Justin has followed in his commitment to service. Usher has also taught his protégé about the importance of charity through his own philanthropic organizations, including New Look, which provides educational resources for people in need and tackles urban-renewal projects.

46
SCHOOLS

The number of schools that Pencils of Promise has built and secured funding to build—much of it with the help of Beliebers!

also be donated to charity.

Many of the charity organizations with which Justin works closely involve helping children. In addition to Pencils of Promise, he is aligned with the Make-A-Wish Foundation, which grants "wishes" to hospitalized children, many of whom suffer from terminal diseases. He often visits with its children at his concerts and in hospitals. "It's just crazy that I'm a wish," he told CNN.

He has also worked with It Gets Better, a nonprofit organization raising awareness and providing counsel for victims of bullying, and has helped join the movement to warn against the often fatal consequences of texting and driving. "Every night we perform, we have a banner that goes up that says 'Don't Text and Drive,' so it really means a lot to me," Justin said to MTV News. The performer also appeared on an episode of the original giving-back program, *Extreme Makeover:*

Justin Bieber performs in 2010 at the BET-SOS Saving Ourselves Help for Haiti Benefit Concert in Miami, Florida.

Chapter 15:
JUSTIN GIVES BACK

Home Edition, benefitting a family who lost their daughter to texting and driving and now spearheads their own campaign against the dangerous practice.

He has also harnessed the power of online auctions like eBay to get much-needed money to good causes. A pair of rhinestone-embellished Supras sold on eBay to benefit the Ovarian Cancer Research Fund. Proceeds from that famed lock of hair raised more than $40,000 for a variety of charitable organizations.

Recently, he has partnered with Give Back Brands to develop his fragrance, Someday. One hundred percent of net proceeds from the perfume sale will go straight to multiple charities. "SOMEDAY

> ### QUOTABLE *JUSTIN*
>
> *"It's really important that I'm able to help out other kids. I'm a kid myself, so it means a lot to me,"*
>
> **—Justin to MTV News about his partnership with Pencils of Promise.**

is the idea that we can change the world, make our dreams come true, and even be with the one person that means everything," said Bieber. "Giving back has always been incredibly important to me, but let's be honest.... I wanted to create a fragrance for my female fans that I can't get enough of...that I want to get next to and I can't stay away from. I know they'll love the scent, but also the opportunity to support some amazing charities. It's a gift that gives back."

There are myriad causes and organizations to which Justin has contributed his attention—too many to name here. One thing is for certain: in a short time, he has established a considerable legacy for himself.

"For me it goes past the money," he told

JUSTIN REACHES OUT

Unscramble the letters below to read the secret message.

JUNSIT "WHOSS SHI THERA" OT LOPPEE NI EDEN

Answer: Justin "shows his heart" to people in need. Spurring the campaign to help the three Berry children, who lost their parents and two of whom were paralyzed in a tragic accident in July 2011, Bieber recruited celebrities from Lady Gaga to Britney Spears to Katy Perry. The performers took to Twitter to tell the story of the Berry children and raise funds for the Berry family.

Justin Bieber performs at the Justin Bieber concert to benefit College Track at The Mountain Winery on June 11, 2011, in Saratoga, California.

Singers Celine Dion, Gladys Knight, Justin Bieber, Usher, Kristian Bush, Barbra Streisand, LL Cool J, Harry Connick Jr., Wyclef Jean, Vince Vaughn, Jeff Bridges, Toni Braxton, and others at the "We Are the World 25 Years for Haiti" recording session held at Jim Henson Studios on February 1, 2010 in Hollywood, California.

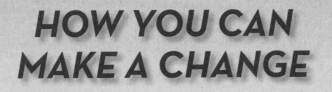

HOW YOU CAN MAKE A CHANGE

Most fans of Justin Bieber have already made contributions to charity, whether it's through buying albums, attending concerts, or getting the word out about some of the causes close to the celeb's heart via Twitter and Facebook. But there's so much more to be done. Volunteer opportunities are available in every town across the nation, including yours! Not sure where to start looking? Here's a place to start.

Do Something: According to its official Web site, "DoSomething.org is one of the largest organizations in the U.S. that helps young people rock causes they care about.... By leveraging the web, television, mobile, and pop culture, DoSomething.org inspires, empowers and celebrates a generation of doers...who recognize the need to do something, believe in their ability to get it done, and then take action." Visit DoSomething.org for help in finding the right cause for you, putting together a guide for action for a cause close to your heart, and sharing your passion with other doers.

Serve.gov: Spurred by President Obama's "United We Serve" initiative, calling Americans everywhere to serve in their communities, this Web site helps unite organizations in need

with people who want to help. The site also provides a forum for charities and people to post their own projects and recruit more volunteers.

Volunteer Match: This Web site connects organizations in need of volunteers with their communities. Looking for a good place to donate your time and energy? Search VolunteerMatch.com for opportunities in your area.

AmeriCorps.gov: This national organization helps guide individuals in a wide variety of community-service opportunities. Bonus: full-time AmeriCorps volunteers can qualify for grants and loan repayments that can help them pay for college!

Approach local businesses that do something you dig; they might really need your help! Ask your friends and teachers what they're passionate about. Chances are you share a common concern. There's strength in numbers.

Whether it's volunteering at your local humane shelter or hospital, starting a food drive for the homeless, or raising money for families in need in your own community, the power is yours to do something. Don't let your time and energy go to waste!

Chapter 16:

THE FUTURE IS NOW

Justin Bieber's unprecented rise to fame is matched only by his equally unprecedented popularity and mastery of his career. He is nothing short of an international phenomenon.

He is a multiplatinum recording artist, and has scored a #1 album in 17 countries. He is a giant of social media, with truly staggering Internet numbers—more than 1 billion views on YouTube, more than 27 million Facebook fans, and more than 12 million followers on Twitter. He has won music awards from the AMA to the VMA; he took home a Webby for his work on the Internet. He has been named one of *Time*'s most influential people, Barbara Walters' 10 Most Fascinating

> **QUOTABLE** *JUSTIN*
>
> *"I see myself making a smooth transition from being a teenage, um, you know, teenage heartthrob basically to, you know, to an adult singer. I want to make that smooth transition, kind of like Usher or Justin Timberlake did it."*
>
> **—Justin to the Associated Press**

People, and one of *Forbes'* highest-earning celebrities.

A best-selling author, box-office champion, top-earning touring artist, and award-winning philanthropist, he is at the top of his game in every facet of his career. It's a laundry list of achievements most artists wouldn't hope to achieve over the course of their entire careers; Bieber has done it at the age of 17.

Undoubtedly talented, the unique ingredient of humbleness may indeed be the catalyst that has put Bieber over the top. "As long as you have the right mind-set and stay humble and remember to always put God first, I think you can do anything," the singer told Ryan Seacrest.

Being successful in multiple

JUSTIN STOOD HERE!

THEY SAY IF YOU CAN MAKE IT HERE, YOU CAN MAKE IT ANYWHERE. WHEN JUSTIN SOLD OUT MADISON SQUARE GARDEN, HE CEMENTED HIS STATURE AS AN A-LIST PERFORMER, ONE OF FEW WHO CAN SELL OUT THE STORIED VENUE.

Musician Justin Bieber attends the 2011 VH1 Do Something Awards at the Hollywood Palladium on August 14, 2011, in Hollywood, California.

Justin Bieber accepts the Bill Lowery Horizon Award at the 33rd Annual Georgia Music Hall of Fame Awards at the Cobb Energy Performing Arts Center on September 17, 2011, in Atlanta, Georgia.

WHO SAID IT?

A: "I've drummed with Bieber before.... It's obvious this is a person that went from YouTube sensation to viral sensation to international superstar — that's gonna be the next level of celebrity."

B. "He came to sing at [my house]. He's a very nice young man."

C. "I see Justin Bieber and I just want to hug him."

D. "I'm riddled with Bieber Fever."

Answers: A-The Roots' Questlove; B-President Barack Obama; C-Taylor Swift; D-Johnny Depp

pursuits is a rare feat. It takes a massive amount of commitment to get there. Jada Pinkett Smith should know. Her husband leveraged early fame as a rapper and a hugely successful adult recording artist and Oscar-nominated actor. "[Bieber is like] a little Will Smith. He's so passionate about what he does and he does it for his fans," Jada Pinkett Smith said to Chelsea Handler in a recent interview.

Usher thinks Bieber's special-something is more intangible. "He was born a star," the singer told *Time* magazine. "He knew what he wanted to accomplish; all he had to do was get everyone else to believe it.... Stay tuned, because his story will get even better."

"I think he's the kid who [will] go beyond the teenage puppy-love thing; he's the kid that they grow with. He's special," said L.A. Reid in *Justin Bieber: Never Say Never.*

Usher echoes the sentiment. "As he grows, as he goes through life's experiences, as he loves, as he finds

SAY WHAT?

"Justin is here to stay. I think he's got a long career ahead of him."

—Simon Cowell to Teen.com

Chapter 16:
THE FUTURE IS NOW

relationships. All of this will become a part of the story, and for me it's beautiful to watch because I can understand it firsthand. This is something that could definitely be a forever story— only if he wants it."

Manager Scooter Braun agrees. "Watch what happens when Justin's 19," he said. "People forget that Michael Jackson was considered done after the Jackson 5, yet he changed the world," he told the *Hollywood Reporter*.

Justin's team, or "family," as he calls his inner circle, have a professional ambition to see their artist succeed, but they also feel a strong personal commitment to the singer's upbringing. "Ninety percent of my job is making sure he becomes a good man. That's a family," says manager Scooter Braun in *Justin Bieber: Never Say Never*.

Having his road family and his mom with him at every step along the way has been crucial in keeping the musician grounded. The component of faith—Justin leads a

> ## HAIR APPARENT
>
> *By now most people know that Justin's about more than just that mop top. "People are always like, 'So, your hair is your trademark' and stuff. I'm like, 'No. My voice is my trademark, you know?'" he told the Associated Press.*

prayer vigil before each show—is another strong foundation. "I pray all the time. I pray two to three times a day. When I wake up I thank him for my blessings. I thank him for putting me in this position. And at the end of the day I get out my Bible," he explained to the *Guardian*.

Pattie's goal for Justin transcends his career. It's easy to see that she has been a primary influence on his character. "I want Justin to find his identity and worth not from what he can do but from who he is," she said in the movie.

"There are so many people out there who think he's just some kid acting. He's going to be a teen sensation and then he's going to go away. I wouldn't bet against Justin and I sure wouldn't bet against Justin and his team. We like being the underdog... It gives us something to work for," said Scooter Braun in *Justin Bieber: Never Say Never*.

Justin has no plans to hold back. "I know that to be the best I can be will take a lot of work. I know I have to give up a lot of

> ## UNDER THE INFLUENCE
>
> *Both Justin Timberlake and Usher were musicians who successfully made the leap from teenage popsters to adult artists. Little wonder, then, that the two artists were in a near bidding war to sign Bieber to begin with.*

Justin Bieber arrives at the 2011 BET Awards.

Chapter 16:
THE FUTURE IS NOW

myself, or a lot of a private life. But the saying 'Practice makes perfect,' really does make sense. The more you practice, the better you get," Justin told *Vanity Fair*.

When asked what he sees for himself in the future, he said, "I see myself just growing.

TWITTER-PATED:

#beforeihadmyfans i didnt know living my dream was possible. so thank you.

APRIL 10, 2011

I didn't know that any of this was really possible. I grew up in a really small town with not a lot of money, and I liked singing, but it was just something that was a hobby. And as I get into it more, I want to grow as an artist, as an entertainer, and basically perfect my craft. I want to be the best that I can be," he continued.

JUSTIN REACHES OUT

So life isn't completely normal for the superstar, but he isn't complaining. When asked recently whether he ever wished for a normal life, he had an interesting reply. Check out the convo, below:

@gabbygrutt14 gabby gruttadaro
@justinbieber if you could..would you for one day go back to being a normal kid? just for a day #randomquestion

@justinbieber Justin Bieber
@gabbygrutt14 yeah...for more than 1 day. i love my life but yeah. this question stuck out to me. i wanted to answer it. Thanks

@justinbieber Justin Bieber
but i feel really blessed to do what i do. very grateful. i am normal though

As Mama Jan has said time and again, "You gave up normality a long time ago for spectacular—not many people can be that, so enjoy it." By all accounts, it looks like he's doing just that.

Justin Bieber and Usher attends The 53rd Annual GRAMMY Awards held at Staples Center on February 13, 2011, in Los Angeles, California.

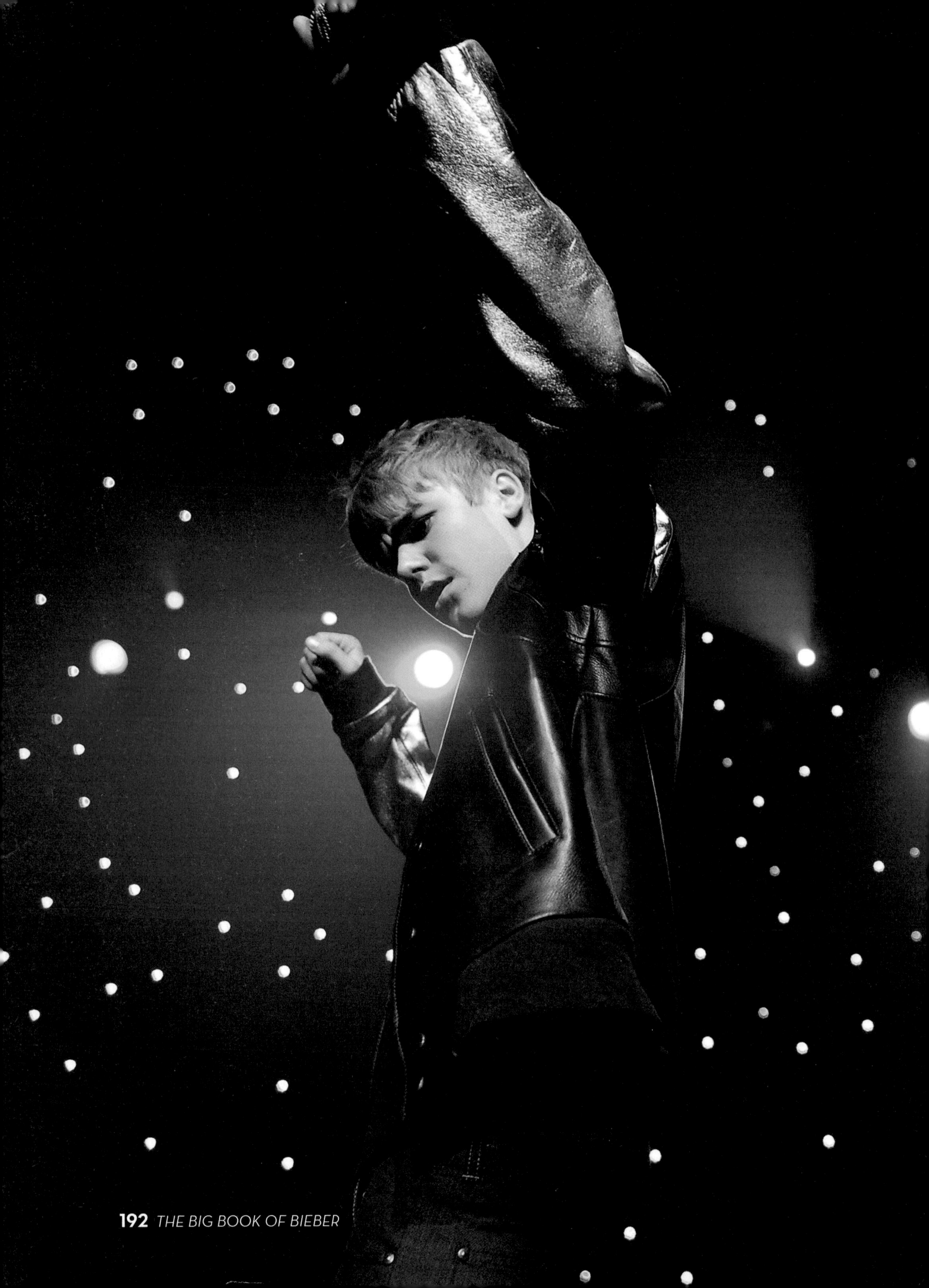